ANTARCTICA

NO SINGLE COUNTRY · NO SINGLE SEA

TEXT CREINA BOND&ROY SIEGFRIED

PHOTOGRAPHY·PETER JOHNSON

MAYFLOWER BOOKS
NEW YORK

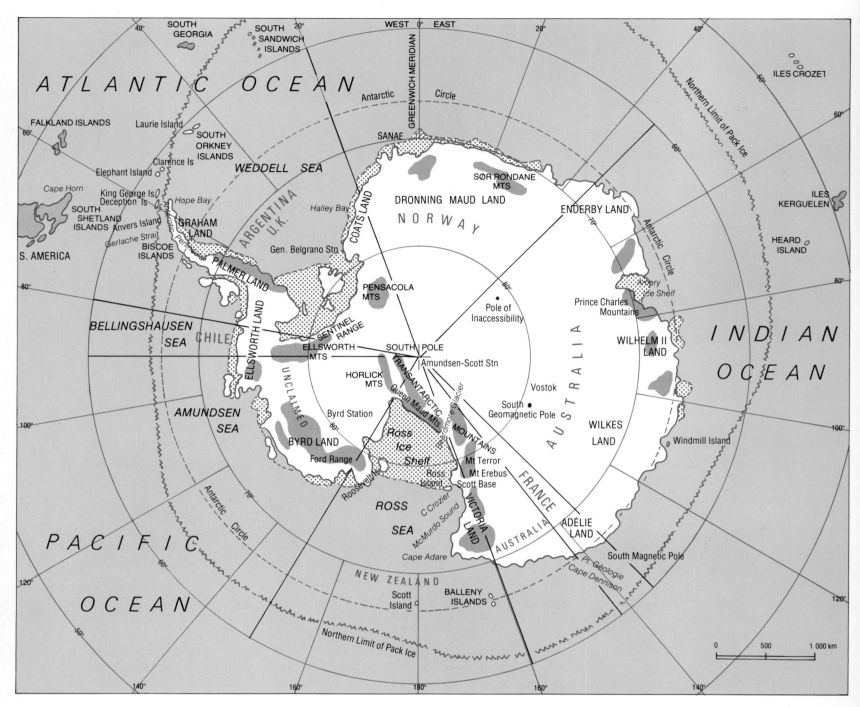

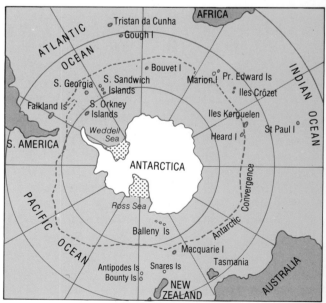

Designed by Walther Votteler, Cape Town
Lithographic reproduction by Hirt & Carter (Pty) Ltd, Cape Town
Photoset by McManus Bros (Pty) Ltd, Cape Town
Printed and bound by Printpak (Cape) Ltd, Cape Town

ISBN 0 8317 0380 6

Manufactured in the Republic of South Africa
First American edition

Foreword

In spite of its inhospitable climate, the Antarctic continent and the seas surrounding it are very important to mankind. It is a region of fantastic beauty and of immense scientific interest. It has a proud history of exploration and contains stores of natural resources, some of them renewable, some non-renewable.

In 1957 at the time of the International Geophysical Year, it seemed likely that the pattern of thoughtless over-exploitation wrought by man over so much of his planet's surface would shortly be extended into the White Continent.

At this juncture a group of far-sighted people from different nations came together to negotiate an international treaty to protect the Antarctic lands from territorial claims and exploitation. This, it was suggested, might be the blueprint for other common heritage areas such as the deep seas and maybe also for the exploration of space.

Whether these high hopes will ever materialise it is perhaps too early to tell, but in the meanwhile the Antarctic Treaty which was ratified in 1961 and holds force for 30 years, has been acceded to by 19 nations including the 13 Treaty member states. It is of the highest importance that the concepts of responsible stewardship should prevail and that immediate economic consideration should not be the only criteria for deciding man's role in Antarctica and its surrounding oceans.

Tourism is likely to be a significant factor in the future and the impact of it on the Antarctic environment and particularly on the colonies of breeding penguins and other birds will have to be carefully watched, though I do not doubt that a way can be found for very many people to enjoy the unbelievable beauty of mountains, clouds, ice and sea without any measurable damage.

I hope this book with its beautiful photographs will help to make all who have not been fortunate enough to visit this continent aware of the significance of it, and enable them to bring pressure to bear on the decision-makers for the safeguarding of its future.

Peter Scott, Slimbridge, April 1979

Introduction

And when there were no more elephant seals to boil, ships took to chasing whales instead. Whales were good for boiling, too. Once peeled of their blubber, the huge unwanted corpses were set adrift on watery cemeteries.

The north grew steadily richer as uncounted cargoes left the Southern Ocean to make lubricants for the new machine age, explosives for war, lipsticks, perfumes, ointments, candles, petfood . . .

Yet this wealth came only from the products of the sea. For when Antarctica was discovered, Cook's prophecy seemed fulfilled: there could be no profit in this new land, this continent without birdsong, creaking and moaning with ice. It is so different from the familiar countries of the earth it could be another planet. The sky swings and whirls with colour. Ice crystals in the air play tricks with the light so that there seem to be not one sun but many suns, there are arcs and haloes and a night with a ring of moons. Lakes of brine explode with the cold. The sea is solid but the solid sea moves, and solid rivers collide with the sea.

Not until 1978 was the first human born among Antarctica's glaciers and icefields; for 121 years before that men died in the snows, their corpses so well preserved in their white graves that they passed into the future unchanged by death.

Antarctica blurs the boundaries of time – yesterday and today are easily confused when the frozen relics of the past 5 000 years drift past in an iceberg. Even the water boiling in the kettle may have been quarried among the blizzards of those long-ago summers when Cook first sailed into the Southern Ocean . . . a cup of coffee may contain water of 1772 vintage.

Because Antarctica knew nothing of man's history, it has given him a chance to escape his past; and because it was remote for so long – a continent without tradition – it provided the freedom to shape a new law. In 1959, 12 nations drafted a contract without precedent. It led to the ratification of the Antarctic Treaty in 1961 – dedicating the continent to peace. Science would be Antarctica's only industry – knowledge would be its trade. And those nations that had raised their flags on its ice-bound shores, agreed to freeze all claims for 30 years.

Yet the Treaty was incomplete, for it concerned itself chiefly with the mainland, keeping the Southern Ocean beyond the law. And the Treaty had another blemish, for it assumed no profit could accrue from Antarctica.

Nonetheless, for 20 years the Treaty has maintained its promise. Countries at each other's throats elsewhere, have found in the south a place to work together, to co-operate in extending the frontiers of science. But now cracks have appeared and the Treaty is under strain. Coal, oil, gas and base metals are all possibilities – and krill is a potential harvest from the sea. Indeed, the amount of krill that could be netted from the Southern Ocean every year could equal that of all the fish caught in the rest of the world.

Can it be done, though, without knocking a hole in the ocean? Krill is more than just food for penguins – it is food for millions of other birds, millions of seals, thousands of whales – it is a major link in the food webs of the cold Antarctic waters.

For 50 years scientists have been at work in the Southern Ocean, but 50 years has not been long enough for wise answers. 'We do not have adequate information,' says a recent document prepared by several international Antarctic research committees. 'Despite past research activities we have only very rough estimates of krill stocks. Critical aspects of the biology and ecology of krill remain to be clarified.'

Haunted by past tragedies, scientists around the world are joining in an international research programme, BIOMASS, which hopes to ensure that the Southern Ocean can be used with wisdom, and used forever.

Even as the scientists begin their work, trawlers from a number of nations are busy in the south. Already Russian and Polish housewives are buying Antarctic fish. Japanese and Chileans are tasting krill.

Deadline for the first BIOMASS results is the mid-1980's. But will businessmen and politicians wait until then?

Treaty nations with claims to Antarctic land are believed to be demanding that their sovereignty be recognized so that they will have jurisdiction over the adjoining sea. And even as the Treaty powers argue over who is entitled to what, 'outside' nations are claiming their share of the Southern Ocean too.

No home was ever built on the high seas. No civilization ever grew from the waves. Where there are no fences, there can be no ownership, and where there is no owner, there can be no love.

12

6   7

2 What's the Use

'Polar exploration is at once the cleanest and most isolated way of having a bad time which has ever been devised,' said Apsley Cherry-Garrard who went south with the ill-fated Captain Scott in 1910. 'It is the only form of adventure in which you put on your clothes at Michaelmas, and keep them on until Christmas, and save for a layer of natural grease, find them as clean as though they were new. It is more lonely than London, more secluded than a monastery, and the post comes but once a year . . .'

Or once every two years, or perhaps even three years. In those days when a sailing ship disappeared behind the green swells of the Southern Ocean it lost contact with the world; radio was not yet known. A ship passed out of sight into silence, sometimes for a summer, sometimes for ever. Outside the harbour there was no way to summon help, signal disaster, receive messages or announce a change of plan. Between 1820 and 1822 alone, seven ships vanished.

Not that there could be much planning about a trip south. Antarctica's coast is an erratic one, with shores that wander out to sea, and ramble back again. Mountains shift, peaks stray and even the plains are mobile. The sky is afloat with mirages, and the clear air so confuses perspectives that crags 300 kilometres distant appear close by. A ship's course might be planned on paper, but the ice directs its journey – with shoves, nudges and blockages often taking it a very different route.

Was there solid ground anywhere, early sailors wondered, or only phantom coasts and prowling ice?

In 1820 an American sealing captain, Nathaniel Palmer, looked across 'a sea filled with Immense Icebergs' to 'a shore everywhere perpendicular'. It was not welcoming but it was definitely 'land'.

For more than 40 years sealers had been risking their ships among the floes, but from 1819 a note of national rivalry sounded across the southern waters. That was the year Captain Thaddeus von Bellingshausen of the Imperial Russian navy left Kronstadt intent on making discoveries as close as possible to the South Pole. He followed the ice around Antarctica, unaware that he was following the outline of an unknown continent. His voyage was a scientific success, but the tsar was disappointed. He had hoped for something more than new charts and pages of meticulous observations. Resentfully he said it would be too expensive to publish von Bellingshausen's maps. And that was that. More than 130 years would pass before Russians returned to Antarctica.

While von Bellingshausen may have been unpopular with his ruler, he was never as controversial as Jules Dumont D'Urville, a remarkable French navigator who led the next national expedition into the floating icefields in 1837.

'This old fellow won't take us far,' he overheard a sailor say as he took command of his two ships, the *Astrolabe* and *Zelée*. The remark must have rankled in a man plagued with gout and an uncertain temper. D'Urville had joined the French navy at 16, more interested in voyages of discovery than warfare, of which he disapproved. He had undoubted ability and his talent and energy took him to the top. At 51 he was an admiral. However, he was a hostile and outspoken critic of the naval establishment, and when he died his colleagues were so glad to see the last of him that his tomb was inscribed with the words: *No mourning, a little ash, a little earth, a lot of fuss.* (This was later to be erased.)

Although not particularly interested in Antarctica, D'Urville accepted the command of the French expedition because 'when I examined the proposal from every aspect I came to the conclusion that an attempt to reach the South Pole would appeal to the public as something so novel, so great and even astounding that it could not fail to attract attention'.

La gloire! That was what the South Pole offered, and that was all the French king was interested in. D'Urville's instructions were very simple: To go farther south than anyone had been before.

In January 1840 the Frenchmen sighted an icebound coast. Unable to make a landing below the shiny cliffs they did the next best thing – they sent a boat to a rocky islet nearby where the tricolour was raised before a watching crowd of penguins. D'Urville, a good family man, named the place Adélie Land 'to perpetuate the memory of my profound regard for the devoted companion who has three times consented to a long and painful separation in order to allow me to accomplish my plans for distant exploration'. These little penguins were to carry his wife's name too.

Not long afterwards the French ships were hove-to in a drifting fog when a strange vessel, an American man-of-war, passed within hailing distance. Alone among the icebergs in a desolate wilderness, the ships ignored each other. Later each commander would accuse the other of the snub.

Lieutenant Charles Wilkes was the commander of the American ship, one of five in the United States Exploring Expedition dispatched to the Antarctic in 1838.

Long before he left home he was feeling gloomy about the trip: 'It required all the hope I could muster to outweigh the intense feeling of responsibility that hung over me. I may compare it with that of one doomed to destruction,' he said. There was bungling before they set sail – quarrels, resignations, delays and desertions. The expedition was badly planned and badly equipped: when the Americans stopped over in Australian harbours, the Australians 'considered us doomed to be frozen to death'. Wilkes's own ship, *Vincennes*, had large gun ports which, while hardly necessary for guns, since the expedition was not planning to shoot anybody, let in large quantities of icy sea spray.

Wilkes was not to blame for his leaky, rotting vessels. In fact only his iron determination – and frequent repairs – carried them through several summers in the ice. Whenever there was an opportunity, however, his men deserted in droves. Wilkes was a tough skipper and his subordinates loathed him so much that when he finally sailed into a home port, he found no hero's welcome but a court martial. Some of the charges against him – such as wearing a uniform to which he was not entitled – were ridiculous, but he was convicted on one count of illegally punishing his men, and reprimanded.

And if that was not enough, he was to be further discredited when his sightings of land around Antarctica were proved false by the very next expedition south.

Yet to be fair to the man, the material brought back from his unhappy cruises helped to influence the establishment of the Smithsonian Institution. And he was the first to state firmly that the land he saw was 'the Antarctic continent'.

In 1839, Sir James Clark Ross, 'the handsomest man in the Navy', led a British expedition in HMS *Erebus* and HMS *Terror*. He was 'a Captain devoted to the cause of Marine Zoology and constantly on the alert to snatch the most trifling opportunity to add to our collections,' said Joseph Hooker, the enthusiastic young botanist who doubled as assistant surgeon on the historic voyage.

Terror and *Erebus* had been adapted for working in the ice, and the crews were hand-picked men. The British government even provided equipment for the study of natural history: 25 reams of paper, two 'botanizing' vascula, and two cases for bringing home live plants. But that was all. Not an instrument, not a book, not a bottle. Rum from the ship's stores was the only preservative. That, and salt water. The ship's botanist did not even have a table to work on, but Ross invited him to share his cabin, and science advanced.

'So prolific is the ocean that the naturalist need never be idle,' said Hooker, 'not even for one of the 24 hours of daylight during a whole Antarctic summer.' Below the ship flowed patches of discoloured water: green, red and brown plankton soups that choked the nets swung overboard. And in the underside of floes, stained the yellow of rotten melons, Hooker recognized diatoms – a further sign of the rich fecundity of the sea. Smooth-backed whales surfaced around the ship, blowing misty columns of spray. Seals dozed on passing floes, while penguins advanced curiously across the ice.

As the midnight sun circled above the masts, and 'growlers' thumped against the ship, Hooker recorded each new discovery: 'Almost every day I draw,' he said, 'sometimes all day long till two or three in the morning, the Captain directing me; he sits on one side of the table, writing and figuring at night, and I on the other, drawing. Every now and then he breaks off and comes to my side to see what I am after. As you may suppose we have had one or two little tiffs, neither of us being helped by the best of tempers, but nothing can exceed the liberality with which he has thrown open his cabin to me and made it my workroom at no little inconvenience to himself.'

Large collections of marine organisms accumulated. 19

15

16

17

Jawbones of Rock

was 4 000 metres thick. Under the burden, the earth's crust dented. Parts of Antarctica sagged 1 000 metres.

Much of this is guesswork, of course, but since the 1950's there have been big advances in reconstructing the continent's past. Antarctica's historians are relatively new arrivals. In 1956 there was only one research station on the mainland. In 1957, 12 nations marked the International Geophysical Year (IGY) by sending teams of scientists to occupy the uninhabited continent, and where there had been one station, soon there were 40. The era of scientific exploration was underway. With sophisticated technology the limits of earth, sea and ice were separated for the first time – on paper, anyway. Blank maps acquired features. Statistics piled up like drift before a blizzard. Books and journals bulged with new information; pages and pages of data accumulated.

Right from the start it was obvious science was on the brink of important revelations. Antarctica had evidence for continental drift.

Geologists were the first to find the clues in the faces of rock cliffs free of ice. Congealed in the rock were wavy bands of dark shales, brown-grey sandstones, fine-grained dolerite. And there was something immediately familiar about the profiles: the rock poking through the ice resembled the hills of South Africa and South America more than 3 000 kilometres away.

'Literally astonishing . . . without parallel,' ran one report of that period. Like slices from the same cake, the rocky layers of Antarctica, South America and South Africa made a startling fit when compared side by side.

'The similarities have become stronger with each season's fieldwork in recent years,' H. J. Harrington reported in 1965 in one of the first volumes on Antarctic research. 'They have had a profound effect on some Australasian geologists who have been traditionally very sceptical of continental drift theories, but have had to contemplate them after seeing the Antarctic sequences.'

Fossil plants were to convert some doubters, too. Over the years new collections of fossil ferns, cycads, horsetails and trees had been added to the samples Scott and his men dragged on that sledge in 1912. Antarctica's ancient plants also seemed familiar – in fact the fossil floras of Africa, Australia, India and South America were practically the same. Palaeobotanist Edna Plumstead placed them all 'without question in a single Gondwana floral province'.

The evidence was convincing but not yet conclusive. After all, argued the unbelievers, the propagules of plants could have drifted across the oceans. Similar floras were not necessarily proof that the continents had been one.

The ghostly imprint of ancient magnetism added to the story being deduced from rock: when rocks are formed they adopt the prevailing magnetism of the earth. Antarctica's rocks, like fossil compasses, showed that 165 million years before, the Antarctic Peninsula had been in the sub-tropics, while the eastern part of the continent had been at a latitude of 40° south.

Even as the arguments for continental drift grew stronger, the case had one outstanding flaw. If Antarctica and Africa had been one country – not only would they have had plants in common, they would have had animals, too. Nowhere on Antarctica had anybody found evidence that animals had ever walked that now frozen land.

Then in December 1967 a New Zealand geologist, Peter J. Barrett, chipped a small fragment of a fossil lower jaw from the slopes of Graphite Peak in the central Transantarctic Mountains. Newspapers around the world headlined the find. Although the fossil was too incomplete for proper identification, there was no doubt that it belonged to a labyrinthodont amphibian – one of the first vertebrate animals to have walked on land some 230 million years ago. Here was the first indication that once upon a time Antarctica had been inhabited by land-living animals. But did it prove anything about continental drift?

Still the unbelievers argued that the owner of the fossil jaw might have reached Antarctica by swimming across the sea. Modern amphibians cannot tolerate salt water – but perhaps the oceans were not as salty 230 million years ago. It was easier to theorize about marvellous jaunts *via* winds or logs, than to believe in continents drifting.

The evidence of that fragment of jaw had such implications, however, that in 1969 a team of 20 scientists arrived in Antarctica to intensify the fossil hunt. It was the stormiest spring in years and howling gales kept the men in their tents for a month before they were airlifted up into the high mountains. They began their work on the low cliffs of an outlying peak called Coalsack Bluff. Temperatures were below freezing, and they had to crouch close to the rock as wind-driven snow tore past. Yet, on the first day, they uncovered 30 fossils.

On the twelfth day came the big find – a fossil skull. The shape entombed in the barren rock was no stranger to the men who uncovered it, but a familiar creature called *Lystrosaurus*. With large eyes and nostrils placed near the top of its head, *Lystrosaurus* was a lizard-like animal the size of a dog, and was once common in Africa and India – so common, in fact, that the diverse animals found in rocks of that period go by the name of *Lystrosaurus* fauna. Before the fossil hunters had finished their hammering at Coalsack Bluff, they had found many companion creatures that resembled the fauna of the African Karoo.

Could *Lystrosaurus* have evolved on two continents 3 000 kilometres apart? Could coincidence account for the likenesses between whole collections of animals? The fossils of the reptile proved beyond doubt that Africa and Antarctica had long ago been one.

Even before the new finds were announced, however, the theory of plate tectonics provided a mechanism to explain how masses of land had travelled across the sea. Antarctica had never been self-propelled. Slow-flowing currents of hot rock deep inside the earth had carried the continent from the warm sub-tropics to the South Pole.

19

20 21

change, accurate records of years when the world was wetter, drier, colder, warmer, dustier, cleaner.

At Camp Century, Greenland, the drills touched bedrock at 1 300 metres. At Byrd Station, Antarctica, the drills went farther – 2 300 metres. Few events in polar research caused as much excitement as those first deep cores.

By the 1970's the grinding drill would no longer be a novelty. All over Antarctica ice cores would be lifted out and shipped, deep frozen to laboratories for analysis. Past temperatures would be calculated from the oxygen composition of each layer. And eventually, like the oozes, the cores of ice would also reach cold rooms where their rows would be testimony to the growth of a new science.

Every lump of ice that is bored is an age in history. The first metre from the surface takes you back 20 years. Farther down you touch snow that fell the year Copernicus put the sun in the centre of the heavens. Below that you can reach the heyday of the pharaohs, and deeper still a year when Neanderthal man was sharpening his flints.

Near the Pole of Inaccessibility, the point most remote from all the coasts of Antarctica, a hole has reached a depth of 1 000 metres. Bedrock lies another 2 500 metres on. The ice from the 950 metre level has already been determined as 51 000 years old.

As the programme of ice-core drilling has expanded, so it has become an international effort. For two summers recently 36 scientists from six nations waited on the Ross Ice Shelf while a drill tried to penetrate the ice to an undersea world never observed by man. The sunless waters beneath the shelf have been hidden by ice for at least 120 000 years.

In December 1977 a flame jet used for cutting granite melted through 420 metres of ice, and a TV camera was lowered through the hole to give man his first sight of life in the lost world of perpetual darkness. Near the sea bed swimming organisms, which appeared to be tiny fish, drifted across the field of vision. Some creatures were trapped and hauled up to the surface – the largest of them amphipods, little animals in jointed armour.

A specialist in copepods filtered 1 000 litres of sea water that had come from the murky depths without finding any of these tiny planktonic animals – only fine organic debris. 'The first results were disappointing to some,' says biologist Joel Hedgpeth. 'On second thoughts, perhaps these results should have been expected. There was no sign of burrowers or sedentary animals of the sort that feed on plant material, but only of wandering scavengers – the sort of animals seen elsewhere in apparently barren parts of the sea.'

Glaciologists knew there was water below the apparently solid Ross Ice Shelf. But their drills also met water 2 300 metres under the ice on the bedrock below Byrd Station. The base of the ice sheet was at melting point. 'What happens to this water?' asked geologist John Hollin. 'Does it form rivers or a film? In the latter case it must tend to detach the ice from its bed and may be the cause of the catastrophic "surges" which have been observed in ice caps and valley glaciers.'

If part of the Antarctic ice sheet peeled off its base and hurtled free, we could have the trigger for the ice ages of the world.

A. T. Wilson first put forward this theory of the ice ages. He suggested that the Antarctic ice cap was unstable, that it built up until it began to melt at its base, and then 'surged' out to form a large floating ice shelf on the Southern Ocean.

Little is known about 'surges', and nothing definite is known of their causes. More than 40 'surges' have been reported from glaciers in North America alone. The fastest measured was 170 metres a day. If the ice in the centre of the Antarctic ice sheet surged at that velocity, it would reach the coast in only 40 years – a moment in geological time. And John Hollin estimated that an Antarctic surge could cover the sea with ice 200 metres thick, as far as 55° south.

But did 'surges' ever happen? If a massive Antarctic slippage caused the ice ages, there should be signs that the sea level rose rapidly but briefly in the northern hemisphere. So far most of the evidence indicates that it did.

Scientists are now testing the possibility of 'surges' on mathematical models. And at the same time they are trying to work out the annual mass balance of the ice sheet. Is ice building up in the centre of the continent, ready for another surge? Is the ice sheet showing signs of strain? Or is the problem a different one – is the ice melting away?

Along the coast, mountain peaks have glacial scratches on their shoulders, and beaches raised above the sea show that the ice extended farther in the past.

The behaviour of the Antarctic ice cap could provide an early warning of climatic change – but is there a way to understand the behaviour of such an immense, uninhabited, barren mass of ice?

From jigsaw pieces of data it is calculated that 12 500 000 square kilometres of ice cover the continental base rock; 1 500 000 square kilometres make up the floating ice shelves, while the sea fluctuates between about 4 000 000 square kilometres in summer and up to 25 000 000 square kilometres in winter. But it is the volume or mass of these enormous areas of ice that is important in calculations aimed at understanding 'surges'. Each year 1,4 trillion tonnes of ice break off at the edge of the ice cap. And each year 2 000 billion tonnes of fresh snow replenish the continental ice. More or less. Stakes in the ice can show how much snow has settled – but do not show the snow that has blown away. The frequent and prolonged blizzards in Antarctica make it difficult to measure snowfall.

Add the new stuff, subtract the old – it is a rough, uncertain, unsatisfactory equation. The answer varies. There is no acceptable answer yet.

Even as men tussle with their statistics, snow is falling in Antarctica, flake following flake, settling and hardening and one day becoming ice. And within the white drift is the imprint of temperature, traces of chemicals from factories across the world, and the tell-tale signs of carbon dioxide and other pollutants which might be contributing to warming the earth and melting the ice.

Our todays are being stockpiled for tomorrow.

28

29

5 The Second Circle of Hell

Shackleton's men had been working on the ice, dragging stores, when the bad weather blew in. Inside the hut Shackleton worked on finishing touches to his plans for reaching the Pole. Outside the hut temperatures plummeted, and fingers and faces were frostbitten. Several men went in to remind their leader that it was growing very cold. Absorbed in his work, Shackleton just nodded and smiled. As it became steadily colder and windier, however, the men could bear it no longer. A spokesman was sent in to protest, his Balaclava white with snow, his beard frosted, ice splinters sticking to his skin.

'It's blizzing Boss,' he said. 'The wind's increasing, dark snow clouds are working up and some of us are getting frostbitten.' Shackleton smiled, turned up a passage in the Bible that lay on his table and handed it over.

'Read that,' he said.

The man read aloud: 'Many are called but few are chosen.'

'Read again,' said Shackleton. Then he shut the book and said sternly, with the faintest gleam of humour in his eye:

'Many are cold but few are frozen.'

Antarctica is the coldest continent in the world. Even when the midsummer sun is circling the sky, air temperatures seldom rise above freezing. The cold makes rope hard as iron, canvas as rigid as sheet metal. It burns men's skin and splits their teeth. At the South Pole men can seldom leave their skin exposed for more than a few moments without it blistering. The mean annual temperature is -55 °C, a temperature which freezes oil into jelly. Yet that seemed almost tropical to the men stationed at Vostok, a Russian station on the high interior plateau. Here, 3 488 metres above sea level the temperature has dived to a world record low of $-88,3$° C, and men never move outside without being swathed in furs, masks across their faces, and carrying pocket-sized heaters to warm their hands, feet and chests. At temperatures below -80 °C they are allowed outside for periods of only 15 minutes at a time. When it is lower than -85 °C, outdoor trips are limited to 10 minutes.

'In this sort of cold, if you try to burn a candle the flame becomes obscured by a cylindrical hood of wax,' said John Bechervaise: 'If you drop a steel bar it is likely to shatter like glass, tin disintegrates into loose granules, mercury freezes into a solid metal, and if you haul up a fish through a hole in the ice within five seconds it is frozen so solid that it has to be cut with a saw.'

Yet it is the wind, more than the cold, which makes Antarctica dangerous. If the air is still, men at coastal stations can strip to the waist and sunbathe on a clear day despite temperatures below freezing. But the moment a breeze stirs, they have to cover up. A mild wind moving at five metres a second, combined with a still-air temperature of -30 °C will freeze exposed flesh in a minute or less.

A windless day is rare in Antarctica. Only on the high plateau, at places like Vostok, is the air relatively calm, moving lightly along the slopes of the ice dome. At the steep edges of the mountains, however, the wind suddenly accelerates, clouds of snow fly into the air, and under its own weight it blasts down to the coast and out to sea. There the land winds bump into depressions hurtling 2 000 kilometres a day eastwards.

According to the thirteenth-century Italian poet Dante, all those who had committed carnal sin are tossed about ceaselessly by the furious winds of the Second Circle of Hell. On earth the corresponding hell is found in the Southern Ocean.

Here the winds chase each other continuously around the world, driving huge swells that set ships bobbing like corks. Even on relatively calm days the swell can be awesome. 'At one moment it seems impossible that the great mountain which is overtaking the ship will not overwhelm her,' wrote a man on board the *Terra Nova* in 1911. 'At another it appears inevitable that the ship will fall into the space over which she seems to be suspended to crash into the gulf which lies below.' In days of storm, rollers 30 metres high surge endlessly over the horizon.

The Second Circle of Hell

These latitudes are called the roaring forties, the filthy fifties and the screaming sixties. Early sailors dreaded the winds that might capsize their ships and bury them in water.

Nobody kept a tally of the vessels found floating keel up, without survivors, nor is there a count of the ships lying on the bottom of the sea. In 1849 one captain reported seeing two upturned wrecks in a day although 'the wind was blowing too strongly to examine them'.

Even today, modern freighters can founder crossing the stormbelt of the Southern Ocean. The Antarctic Pilot, a guide for mariners, warns that navigation in the area is rendered difficult by 'sudden, violent and unpredictable changes in the weather'. Between sliding walls of grey water ships lurch so dangerously that strong men strap themselves in their bunks and pray, their innards slopping to each roll.

Hundreds of kilometres above the ocean, satellites photograph disturbances in the air – white swirls of cloud that mark the track of growing storms. And from their easy chairs South Africans hear radio and television announcers report: 'A low pressure belt is situated to the south west of the continent, and it is expected that cold, moist air will feed in over the southern part of the country tonight bringing rain and plummeting temperatures.' Those gyrating masses of air may be many thousands of kilometres distant, but they mean bad weather is on the way. All the southern hemisphere feels the influence of polar ice.

On Antarctica itself there are no reliable forecasts. Because the distances between stations are so vast, entire weather systems go undetected. But for those living on the continent there is a rough but usually accurate rule: the weather is consistently bad, and the wind persistently blows.

When Australian explorer Douglas Mawson landed at Cape Dennison in 1912 there was nothing to warn him of the bad times that lay ahead. Rocky spits of land jutted into the sea – low rocks that made an easy landing place on the precipitous coast of Adélie Land. That is what attracted the party as they offloaded stores and hammered up the wooden walls of their huts.

It was not long, however, before they discovered Cape Dennison lay in the zone of collision of air masses moving from both land and sea. They were living in the windiest place in the world.

Over the next two years the average wind speed was 80 kilometres an hour – gale force – and the men developed the art of 'hurricane walking', crampons lashed to their boots, leaning so far into the wind they appeared to be in danger of falling on their faces.

'Picture drift so dense that daylight comes through dully, though the sun may be shining in a cloudless sky,' said Mawson. 'The drift is hurled screaming through space at a hundred miles an hour and the temperature is below zero Fahrenheit. You have then the bare, rough facts concerning the blizzards of Adélie Land. The actual experience of them is another thing. Shroud the infuriated elements in the darkness of a polar night and the blizzard is presented in severer aspect. A plunge into the writhing stormwhirl stamps upon the senses an indelible and awful impression seldom equalled in the whole gamut of natural experience. The world a void, grisly, fierce, appalling.'

In Antarctica rock is polished, scooped into hollows, grooved by the wind. Snowdrifts are sculpted into iron-hard waves called *sastrugi*. Plains are humped into frozen rollers. Ice sheets are blown clean – or buried. Anything movable has to be lashed to the ground or weighted with ice blocks. Even then, aeroplanes break free of their moorings and are wrecked. A man hanging onto a rope is blown out straight, like a flag. The wind blinds him and disorientates him, so that he can lose himself within metres of his camp.

Yet while the wind damages, inhibits and obliterates life – it has other results. In spring its blast clears bays of ice, opening up nesting beaches for penguins. More important, the wind delivers streams of tiny animals, seeds, spores and portions of living plants to 'seed' the isolated islands of the Southern Ocean, dispersing fragments of life on the inhospitable shores of Antarctica. Over thousands of years the wind has been an agent for colonization.

To survive, however, most of the life in the south must hide from the wind. The largest terrestrial carnivore on Antarctica – a mite one millimetre wide – lives so close to the ground that the force of the wind passes it by. Other land animals are just as tiny – they have to be studied with the aid of a magnifying glass in the shelter of rock crevices or banks of moss where they find protection. The plants that manage to grow at the edge of the continent have leathery skins and crouching forms. Seals find windbreaks in a hump of ice, and doze as snowdrifts build up around them.

But if you cannot hide from the wind, you ride the wind. Wherever the westerlies gust across the Southern Ocean, myriads of birds go with them. The more familiar waters of the world have never had such gatherings of seabirds, hovering and fluttering, buoyant on the wind. Gliding albatrosses navigate the southern seas on windpower, sailing through gales with scarcely a beat of their wings; fulmars soar on upcurrents, while thousands of smaller birds range over the waves in remarkable displays of flying skill.

Tiny prions, or whalebirds, are the most numerous, and sometimes they stretch in all directions from daybreak until dark. 'The erratic gliding flight of these [prions] is the most wild and airy type of flight among all birds,' said ornithologist R. C. Murphy. 'When the air is filled with a flock of whalebirds careening in the breeze, rising, falling, volplaning, twisting, sideslipping above the sea, now flashing their white breasts, now turning their almost invisible backs – they resemble the motes in a windy sunbeam.'

Every wind is a highway in the air, and while the westerlies that patrol the Southern Ocean are the best travelled, other winds flick out across them and these winds, too, are known to the birds. Every year Arctic terns leave their breeding grounds near the North Pole for a 35 000 kilometre round trip to feed among the icebergs of Antarctica. A major body of these terns leaves the African mainland on the last lap south, hitching a ride on the so-called Kerguelen trajectory. A wrong turning in the air can be disastrous, and some terns are swept across the Indian Ocean to Australia and New Zealand, to be whirled and buffeted by many more winds before they straggle onto the pack ice, late.

As the currents of the winds are known to the birds, so are the fluid movements of the sea. Antarctica is surrounded by two concentric rings of water flowing in opposite directions. The inner, narrower ring close to the continent is called the East Wind Drift. And beyond it is a much wider ring, the West Wind Drift. Such is the power of the westerly winds that they move 165 million tonnes of water a second, a volume greater than that transported by any other current. Slowly this immense ring circulates around the southern part of the world, a flood 2 000 kilometres wide, travelling about 20 kilometres a day. Only between the Antarctic Peninsula and South America is its wide sweep interrupted, for a narrow gap separates the continents, a gap spiked with islands.

No part of the Southern Ocean is as crowded as this narrow pass with its confused seas, where the wind agitates the water and spiralling currents bring nutrients from the ocean floor. Here there is fertility for the ocean's pastures, undulating meadows of tiny plants, as light as dust, which directly or indirectly feed clouds of krill – small, shrimplike animals – packs of hunting seals and flurries of birds squabbling in the foam. Here whales hang out – and the whaling ships wait for them.

The tracks of passing cyclones probably determine the position of whale feeding grounds, according to C. W. Beklemishev. Whales are found where krill are abundant, and krill are influenced by the winds in the following way: when a cyclone passes over the ocean, water rises in its centre, and this new, upwelled water brings young krill to the surface, dragging them from the depths where they usually live in their earlier stages. By plotting the tracks of cyclones against whale catches and krill distribution, Beklemishev showed that 'the krill is more abundant and there are more blue and humpback whales in regions where the cyclones are more frequent and stay longer'.

The wind is not the only force working on the Southern Ocean. Even while the westerlies impel an ever-turning circle of water, the earth's rotation and the topography of the ocean are controlling other fluid motions – three great water masses at different depths gliding over each other. Water that is cooled and diluted in high latitudes spreads outwards at the surface and bottom of the ocean, while warm water, which replenishes salt as well as heat, moves inwards in the intervening deep layer.

The upper flow is one of sunlight and ice, a low-saline, shallow stream only 200 metres deep that spills north from Antarctica. It is known as Antarctic surface water. Moving below it, in the opposite direction, is another fluid mass, 2 000 metres deep. This relatively warm layer is often referred to as the circumpolar deep water. The third layer, known as Antarctic bottom water, spreads slowly northwards.

At the Antarctic Convergence the cold Antarctic surface stream meets the somewhat warmer waters of the sub-Antarctic, sinks and then continues its northward flow. Although the Convergence has meanders and eddies on its surface, it is an extraordinarily stable front, almost stationary from year to year.

No southward-bound traveller can cross the Convergence without being aware that there is something different happening about him. First there is a sharp drop in temperature. The wind has a new bite. Everywhere there are flocks of birds, darting and swooping. Clouds thicken and fog settles about the ship. It may begin to snow.

67

The Second Circle of Hell

While the Convergence marks a change in the temperature of the sea water, it marks other differences too. This is the area where sperm whales congregate, although nobody knows why. With all the waters of the Southern Ocean open to them, they gather along the line of the Convergence. Some species of birds tend to predominate south of the Convergence – others to the north. And the ragged line of water that separates birds, keeps species of fish and plankton separated, too. Even the ocean floor reflects the limits of the two water masses far above. For below the cold Antarctic surface water the sea bed is covered with diatomaceous ooze, a yellowish mud full of the almost insoluble silica shells of the microscopic single-celled diatoms that live in the ice-strewn seas.

But the tiny plants and animals that flourish in the warmer water are different, and north of the Convergence the minute calcareous shells of foraminifera, not diatoms, cover the soft mud of the sea bed. The water bodies of the sea may be invisible, but their boundaries are impenetrable barriers to some of the passengers that move within them.

The underlying warm water of the Southern Ocean was first discovered by two astronomers sailing with Captain Cook in 1772-1775. They dropped thermometers overboard to measure the temperature of water streaming with broken ice, and were surprised to find that although it was cold on top, there was a warmer layer underneath.

When the British sent the first of their annual *Discovery* expeditions to Antarctic waters 'you couldn't take a course in oceanography', said Sir George Deacon, one of the scientists on board. 'You had to pick it up as you went along.'

Working on deck at night the *Discovery* team dropped canvas-covered frames down to different depths of the ocean on very long, thin steel wires with very small floats. 'And we watched the way the floats drifted,' said Sir George. 'Of course we had no acoustics, no radio to help detect them, and when there was a storm they all disappeared. But they seemed to go in the direction we more or less expected and that did help!'

In this manner they traced something of the path of the warm deep current from the tropics south to the polar sea.

The third major water mass was the last to be discovered, for it lay beyond the reach of those early instruments dangled overboard. Even today it is a mysterious body of water, and its course is difficult to chart, for it springs from the months of darkness when the sea is as hard as stone.

Sea ice is largely fresh water. The first slurries of ice crystals begin to appear on calm seas in autumn, and as the ice joins and thickens into hard, shiny plates, it squeezes salts from the water. Gradually the salts accumulate, burdening the surface water until it sinks down the continental slope into the permanent blackness of the abyss 4 000 metres below. In that remote place of silence and weak-bodied monsters, the salty streams become one of the slowest and deepest water masses in the world – Antarctic bottom water.

This sunless water creeps sluggishly north to wander over the floor of the earth's oceans. Heavy, inert, it takes centuries to cross the equator, and perhaps centuries more to end its journeyings in the deepest of deep oceanic trenches.

And of course this is not the only cold water that leaks out of the Southern Ocean. When the Antarctic surface water sinks at the Antarctic Convergence, it finds a new level, flowing north. And this flow, too, spirals around the world, underlying the surface waters of the Atlantic, Indian and Pacific oceans, washing upwards against submarine shelves to cool the coastal waters of far away lands.

Birds cannot follow the course of Antarctica's hidden water bodies, but with cues provided by the intricate overlap of surface streams, flocks of fulmars and Cape pigeons navigate to keep themselves in food-rich waters on their seasonal journeys to productive areas such as the seas off the west coast of southern Africa.

With neither beginning nor end, the flowing sea can link isolated, widely-separated events.

On a South African beach the breaking surf gathers up traces of a pesticide which was sprayed on maize fields far inland to destroy maize stalk borer. The traces are taken in by small animals and concentrated up the food chain until eventually they reach another shore. Since 1966 pesticide residues have been found in Antarctic seals and birds.

Pollutants, of course, also travel in the atmosphere, for like the sea, air currents impose continuity. Winds blow in ignorance of national boundaries. When atom bombs were exploded in the 1950's, 1960's and 1970's, radioactive dusts crossed the world on moving air to rain down on Antarctica's ice cap.

The winds show man his world is indivisible. So do the merging boundaries of the sea.

42

43

45 46

6 Living on a Volcano

The warning was shouted from the lookout.

Breakers on the starboard bow!

Breakers? Land ahead? The sailors peered through the mists, their weariness suddenly forgotten. It was five months since they had left France with orders to locate the mythical 'Southern Lands', proceeding if necessary as far as 55° south. Two weeks before there had been a sign of change – they had encountered their first iceberg. Then the ships had run into fog, dense banks of white vapour, pelting sleet. When the sailors could see anything at all, it was a sky of lowering clouds, and foam-crested waves running before the wind. There seemed no end to the dreary sea.

These ships had almost reached their limit of 55° south when, early on New Year's Day, 1739, there came that cry from the lookout and, minutes later, snow-covered cliffs loomed out of the ocean.

For the next 12 days the two ships, *Marie* and *Aigle*, beat to and fro, trying to get close enough to make a landing. But although the commander, Jean Bouvet de Lozier, was a fine seaman, neither his skill nor his determination could get a landing party through the surf. In fact it was all they could do to keep the cliffs in view, as wind and sea buffeted the ships. On the thirteenth day there came a storm so violent that the ships could no longer hold their position offshore and they were forced south-east, away from land, out of sight of that snow-capped headland.

Bouvet and his men hoped they had seen the edge of the southern continent. They never knew they had discovered the loneliest island in the world. Bouvet Island or Bouvetøya takes its name from Bouvet de Lozier and the Norse word *øya* for island.

The Southern Ocean has a thin scattering of islands, tiny specks of land separated by immense spaces of water. And the most isolated speck of all is Bouvet Island, a volcanic cone that rises 1 600 kilometres away from any other land.

For perhaps a million years Bouvet has been alone, wrapped in cloud. But although it is remote from other islands in that windy sweep of sea, Bouvet cannot escape a certain likeness to its far-distant neighbours. And that is true of all the islands of the Southern Ocean – they have different ages, a different history, and yet there are uncanny resemblances.

Some islands are relics of Gondwanaland, left standing in the ocean for many millions of years; others are volcanoes that bubbled from cracks in the ocean floor, lifting their summits in uproar and explosion while the sea boiled around them. The youngest islands broke the surface in clouds of steam only 300 000 years ago, and the floor of the Southern Ocean is still demolishing and rebuilding. There is nothing permanent about its landmarks. In the past the sea has raised islands and swallowed them again. Strange events still occur.

A few years ago a low headland mysteriously appeared on Bouvet Island. Bouvet is an area of deep and hidden tensions. In fact this solitary island marks an underwater crossroads – it stands close to the junction of three plates on the earth's mantle. Here Africa, Antarctica and South America were once joined together as one landmass. Here they split to go their separate ways. And although the continents have gone, the margins of their plates remain a region of stress, and thin wisps of steam drift from below Bouvet's screes.

Bouvet and some other oceanic islands, such as Prince Edward and Gough, are the peaks of mountains on the flanks of the Atlantic-Indian ridge – part of a system of underwater ridges in the world's major oceans.

Running along the axis of the Atlantic-Indian ridge is a large, deep rift valley into which material from the interior of the earth is injected as the continents separate. This material solidifies and is magnetised by the earth's magnetic field, and eventually it moves away from the axis of the ridge. This is referred to as 'sea-floor spreading'. By studying the patterns of magnetisation of the rocks on either side of the ridge axis, sci-

77

entists are able to deduce how fast the continents are drifting – Africa and Antarctica are moving apart at the rate of about two centimetres a year.

Bouvet's new headland could have been caused by an undersea eruption, or it may have been an avalanche triggered by earth tremors. Nobody was there when it happened, for nobody has ever lived on the island. Now and again a ship anchors offshore and, for a few hours or a few days, men scramble among the rocks. Men in helicopters have made quick surveys when the weather has not been too bad. However, the island had no visitors between 1955 and 1958 when a shallow bay vanished to become a platform of jumbled volcanic rock, 650 metres long, 350 metres wide and about 25 metres above sea level.

Long before men knew Bouvet had changed shape, animals had discovered that there was a new parking ground in the middle of the sea. Penguins porpoised through the surf to explore the island's new beaches. Fur seals hauled out onto the platform, and soon new-born pups were yapping and squealing on the rough lava surface. Elephant seals, too, found the new territory and dragged themselves up the beaches to bicker with irritation as they rubbed the itches of moulting hides.

Most of Bouvet is biologically barren. Only two per cent of the island is free of ice. Apart from the new platform there is almost no flat land. Precipitous cliffs drop sheer to the sea. The few narrow beaches are swept by falling stones.

Yet animals seek out this bleak, lonely island. Every summer they navigate through the surrounding desolation of water to emerge among its tumbled rocks. When the first scientists – a party of Norwegians – went ashore in 1927 they recorded scattered fur seals and penguins making use of any suitable coast that could be found. Obviously such animals would have been quick to exploit the new headland when it appeared, but were they the only ones to make use of the unexpected breeding space? Or did stray penguins and seals find it accidentally while swimming past on long-distance wanderings?

Whether or not chance brought animals bumping up against the headland, steadily the populations have multiplied. By 1977 there were more than 7 000 chin-strap and macaroni penguins, 1 000 fur seals and 200 elephant seals. There was even a sparse vegetation. In 1964 visiting British scientists found a conspicuous orange lichen on some boulders, and tufts and patches of moss growing on fine debris and in moist hollows. Even though the tufts of moss were not more than three centimetres in diameter, they sheltered many tiny insects, including two species of Collembola, and mites.

These plants and animals were already familiar to the scientists. Life on Bouvet may be meagre, but it is much the same as that found in the South Sandwich islands, 1 770 kilometres away. Although this distance of sea is enormous, the South Sandwich islands lie in the path of the prevailing westerly winds, which also sweep across Bouvet. With the help of the wind, insects and plants must be able to jump that 1 770-kilometre gap of water. Mosses produce microscopic spores, easily transported over long distances by wind. But the wind cannot explain all the affinities of the islands of the Southern Ocean. Charles Darwin was fascinated by the far south. How had plants and animals ever reached such isolated dots of land he wondered when, in the *Beagle* in 1833, he visited the Falklands. Before the ice had obliterated Antarctica, he speculated, 'a few forms were dispersed to various points of the southern hemisphere by occasional means of transport and by the aid of halting places of existing and now sunken islands . . .'

Sir Joseph Hooker argued differently. The islands must be the remains of huge blocks of land, or mountain chains that had subsided into the sea, said this pioneer of Antarctic botany when he voyaged around the Southern Ocean a few years later. No plants could jump huge spaces of salt water.

The debate between Hooker and Darwin became famous and made many a European academic look at the south with sudden scientific interest.

When HMS *Challenger* sailed into Antarctic waters in the 1870's, there was a young naturalist aboard, H. N. Moseley, and he took the discussion further. 'It is possible that the multitude of seabirds inhabiting the islands and nesting as they do, amongst the herbage, may have been of influence in the matter by transporting seeds attached to their feathers or their feet,' he said. 'Most of the birds are of widely wandering habits.'

Giant petrels and wandering albatrosses are often seen with burrs clinging to their belly feathers. The burrs are produced by *Acaena adscendens*, a red-flowering, shrubby plant that carpets hill slopes on some islands. Brown skuas like to nest among the *Acaena*, and at the end of summer their feathers, too, are often stuck with clusters of ripe seeds.

The *Uncinia* sedges are also plants dispersed by birds. Their seeds are armed with grappling hooks guaranteed to catch hold of any passing transport, and when flocks of sheathbills move onto island grasslands at the end of summer, they soon pick up a covering of hooked seeds.

However, birds are quick to preen off any foreign body that adheres to their plumage – so how many seeds take off on a bird setting out on an ocean crossing? And how many travelling seeds survive being dowsed with salt water when the bird alights on the sea?

Life has been haphazardly scattered among the islands. Yet apparently neither wind nor birds could have spread the Kerguelen cabbage. The Kerguelen cabbage worried Moseley. When early mariners first saw the plant, its thick, fleshy leaves reminded them of the familiar vegetable, so they cooked it and found it tasty. The cabbage became famous as a cure for scurvy – in fact its Latin name, *Pringlea antiscorbutica*, records its value as a source of vitamin C.

Moseley observed: 'Crawling about in the heart of the cabbages and sheltering there are to be found swarms of a curious wingless fly, *Calycopterix moseleyi* . . . It crawls about lazily on the cabbage and lays its eggs in the moisture between the leaves and the heart of the plant. The occurrence of the cabbage with the helpless wingless fly seems proof that the plant was not conveyed to the islands by birds.'

The Kerguelen cabbage is a plant with no near relatives, found only at the Prince Edward islands, the Crozets and Kerguelen – each locality 1 000 kilometres apart, separated by open sea. It is now known that the cabbage and the fly do not appear together on all the islands – but there is still no explanation of how the fleshy cabbage travelled.

Theorising about wild cabbages may have occupied Moseley, but the islands offered other interests to the men aboard HMS *Challenger*.

'I landed with a large party all eager to kill a fur seal,' Moseley wrote, and after the party had found and killed six, he commented: 'It is a pity that some discretion is not exercised in killing the animals. The sealers in Kerguelen kill all they can find.'

Sealers were the first men to live on the islands in the Southern Ocean. Apart from seals, there was little to attract settlers to these outcrops poking from the sea.

Close to Antarctica the islands are silent with rock and snow, their dead craters filled with ice. But even the islands beyond the pack-ice zone are dismal places. There may be a green cover on their cold lava, but they lie in the path of winds that gust day after day at gale force, sometimes blowing over a fetch of 8 000 kilometres. The west coasts of the islands are battered by swells that travel unimpeded in deep water to expend their energy against the sea cliffs. Spray is flung far inland, and only plants that can tolerate the salt survive. To escape the winds, island butterflies have lost their wings and look like grasshoppers, and cushion plants have hard fronts able to withstand the impact of windblown material and the chilling and drying influences of gales.

Within a short distance of the coast, the island cover changes from grassland to alpine snows, and there is great botanical interest in these extremes compressed into a tiny area. There are no trees, and the island weather is terrible. Cloud, fog and overcast skies make a sunny day a rare event. Rain falls more often than not. Sometimes there is sleet and snow. The ground is saturated with water, so boggy that a standing man may find himself sinking with water oozing over his boots. The water seeps into shallow pools, it trickles into small lakes, flows into small streams, tumbles down waterfalls. Water percolates through the green meadows, making floating bogs, waterlogged moss-banks, soggy herbfields. Rocks are always damp, the peaty earth sodden.

'It is impossible to find anything to burn,' observed Moseley. Water drips off every grass blade, and where elephant seals wallow among the tussocks, the wetness is churned into foul-smelling mud. Penguin rookeries are a sea of black slime.

If conditions on shore are miserable – landing through the breaking waves is dangerous. The first sealers were willing to take risks, for when they anchored offshore they heard a distant babble of tongues that rose above the wind and the thundering surf. Penguins screamed and trumpeted incessantly. Massed elephant seals groaned and sneezed and belched. And there was the sound of fur seals, so many seals that the rocks reverberated to their calls.

In 1790 the first tall-masted barques sailed into the Southern Ocean to begin the search for seal colonies. Within 30 years 1 200 000 fur seals had been slaughtered at South Georgia. In the first year of sealing at Macquarie Island, 80 000 pelts were taken, whilst the harvest at the South Shetland islands was 320 000 in two years. Sealers even found Bouvet Island, and

79

Living on a Volcano

although there were not many animals on its forbidding shores, what could be taken was taken.

Gangs of sealers spent the summer living in island caves or rough shelters made of boulders, and sooner or later they explored every cove, cranny, beach and headland. 'In their long beards, greasy sealskin habiliments and grim, fiend-like expressions they look more like troops of demons from the infernal regions than baptised Christian men as they sally forth with clubs to the contest,' went one account of that period.

A man could flay 50 seals a day. The skins were washed in salt water, then laid one on top of another with heavy stone weights to press out the surplus moisture. Finally they were salted and packed in casks. Often, however, the pelts were carelessly prepared. In 1821 the *Pegasus* arrived in London from the Antarctic sealing beaches with thousands of once-silky furs a bubbling stew that had to be sold as fertilizer.

By 1830 a visitor to the South Shetlands, W. H. B. Webster, was reporting: '. . . not a single fur seal was seen by us. Although it was but a few years back since countless multitudes covered the shores, the ruthless spirit of barbarism slaughtered young and old alike so as to destroy the race. Formerly 2 000 skins a week could be procured by a vessel: now not a seal is to be seen.'

When Moseley visited the Southern Ocean, 50 years had passed since the heyday of the sealing industry, yet the islands still had their sealers.

At Heard Island, six wild-looking men, with rifles in their hands, made their appearance on the rocks as soon as the ship entered the bay, reported Moseley. With three-year contracts, 'sometimes a man gets desperate from being in so miserable a place and one of the crew of a whaler said that occasionally a man had to be shot.' The sealers had the skin of only one fur seal for sale. Only one. But they were now on the island not for furs, but for oil: elephant seals were what they were after. And it was easy enough to get these animals. The sealers had only to wait on the island beaches every spring for the breeding bulls to flop ashore, three-tonne monsters full of fat. Soon afterwards the cows returned, gathering in crowded harems, and there was unrest on the beaches as bulls roared at each other. In the midst of the bedlam the pups were born, adding to the pile of snuffling bodies heaped together. Preoccupied with pupping and mating, and later with moulting, the elephant seals offered little resistance to their killers.

Soon the islands were marked with the ruins of this trade. Trough-like hollows in the ground covered empty rookeries where the elephant seals used to lie, and the beaches were strewn with bones. 'There were remains of thousands of skeletons,' said Moseley, 'and I gathered a good many tusks of old males. The bones lay in curved lines, looking like tide lines. . .'

Only on beaches inaccessible to men from the land were elephant seals still to be found in any number, and here men were stationed 'to drive the Elephants from this beach into the sea, which they do with whips made of the hide of the Elephants themselves. The beasts thus ousted swim off, and often haul up on the accessible beaches elsewhere, and there they are killed and their blubber is taken to be boiled down. The males show fight when whipped, and are with great difficulty driven into the sea. They are sometimes treated with horrible brutality.'

Wherever men touched the islands, they damaged them. At Marion Island the *Challenger* party found a huge king penguin rookery three-quarters deserted 'but everywhere strewn with bones of penguins in heaps . . . The sealers probably employed their spare time in making penguin oil and perhaps taking skins which are made up into rugs and mats at the Cape of Good Hope, often only the yellow streaked part of the neck being used. Hence the many bones and the emptiness of the rookery.'

By 1874 island shores were already scattered with bones of southern right whales which were hunted in sheltered bays.

Whalers were eventually to give the Southern Ocean its first towns – scruffy clusters of shacks with belching chimneys and squat fuel tanks. They were makeshift places thrown together with indifference by men who knew their stay was temporary – easily nailed up, easily deserted, too.

South Georgia was the centre of the whaling industry – and therefore perhaps the most famous island in the Antarctic seas. Although Captain Cook had claimed the island for Britain in 1775, his countrymen ignored this outpost of the empire until whaling started. Then Britain's interest was renewed, and no rough-and-ready township went up without British licence.

By 1910, however, this mountainous spine of land was becoming crowded with rival establishments and the British refused further concessions. The whalers, forced to look farther afield, sited the next Southern

Ocean metropolis in an odd place – on the smoking rim of a live volcano.

Sealers named it Deception Island because they had almost circumnavigated its shores without finding a harbour when, unexpectedly, they came across a narrow channel and, sailing through, found themselves in a flooded volcanic crater, and the safest harbour in Antarctic waters. Well, safe from the winds and storms of the open ocean! Steam rose from the water's edge at Deception Island, puffs and wisps of vapour simmered through the black cinders of the beach. Sometimes the volcano grumbled a bit, but not enough to be threatening, and the sheltered site became a favourite sealers' rendezvous.

When a whaling station was established at Deception Island in 1910, an English magistrate arrived to take up residence among the sulphur springs. He was there less to administer justice than to be a symbol of British occupation, and he stayed only in the summer months, when the whalers were busy. It was a strange colony he ruled, where hot cinders smoked beneath hills of ice, and the quiet waters of the bay had uneasy spasms.

In 1924 all the great factory ships were tied up for the winter, with their engines cold, when there was an earthquake and underwater eruption. Helplessly the whaling captains watched the beach break into turmoil. A great piece of crater collapsed with a deafening roar and fell into the sea outside. The harbour waters grew hotter and hotter, but the whaling ships could not raise steam, so they were powerless to move, anchored in a cauldron of boiling water. Fortunately the disturbance was short-lived. The beach steadied, the waters cooled, and only the paint peeled off the ships.

Deception Island was not to be an industrial centre for long. In 1925 whaling ships began breaking their ties with land, processing whales at sea. By 1931 business was so bad that Deception's whaling station closed down and the magistrate departed. The volcano could rumble undisturbed.

Britain may well have continued to neglect her volcano had it not been for the Second World War. In time of war even a crumbling, half-alive volcano can have strategic importance.

At first the Southern Ocean seemed out of reach of the war, its waters too vast, too desolate, too remote from the sounds of fighting. Yet this emptiness, of course, was also its attraction. Raiders, submarines and supply ships could hide up among the uninhabited islands, and even the open seas gave shelter, for they belonged to nobody and they were unpatrolled.

Uneasily the British studied maps of the far south. How could they begin to hunt out an enemy over the distances of those seas? Cruisers and submarines sailed from Cape Town to lie in wait at some of the islands – but the Germans were concealed elsewhere, and throughout the war came and went unseen.

Although it never made the standard history books, Deception Island certainly made the war. One day in 1941 the British navy sailed into the drowned crater at Deception. Because the enemy might have been able to make use of the left-overs of the whaling station, the British ship was under orders to destroy the old fuel installations and coal stocks. Then it sailed away.

A year later another ship anchored in the deserted volcano, and in a short but formal ceremony took possession of the island for Argentina.

'It's mine! It's mine!' the two nations were to cry in an annual event of raising and lowering each other's flags, while Deception just huffed and puffed beneath its snows.

By 1944 the British had decided somebody would have to stay to look after the king's estate, and a meteorological station was set up. Meteorology is one science that has made great advances, thanks to war. Wherever nations claim land in the Southern Ocean today, they populate their territory with men studying the weather.

Long after peace treaties had been signed in Europe, the war of Deception Island went on. In 1947 the Argentinians cocked a snook at the British – they built their own meteorological station. In 1952 the Chileans arrived and did the same. That was going too far. A British naval expedition was despatched to remove all foreign buildings, and two Argentinians who were there at the time were deported. The two ships patrolled the waters of Deception Island until the winter gloom set in.

It was clearly a case for the International Court of Justice, although Deception Island was, of course, just one island out of many over which the rival countries were squabbling. Britain lodged an appeal. Argentina and Chile refused to defend.

In 1967 the volcano expressed its own opinion on the matter. It erupted. Spluttering and hissing, a new islet 1 000 metres long emerged from the waters of the bay. Farther along the coast a chunk of land subsided. Nobody took the hint.

Living on a Volcano

Two years later Deception Island tried again. Early one summer morning the ground trembled underfoot. The only inhabitants on the volcano at the time, five men of the British Antarctic Survey, decided to evacuate – but evacuate where? They were walking along the coast when two columns of vapour were flung from the water. The sky darkened. Bombarded with falling cinders, they took to a derelict whaling hut. When there was a lull they stripped sheets of corrugated iron from the walls, and holding the sheets over their heads, tried to make their way back to the station.

It had gone, wrecked by a flood of water. The eruption had cut fissures in the highest mountain on Deception, and great volcanic bombs, some four metres across, lifted the sheet of ice and set it off on a destructive slide.

With the island shaking, spitting and roaring, the men were lucky to be rescued the same day – by the enemy. Helicopters from a Chilean rescue vessel carried them to safety.

Large shocks continued to shudder beneath the crater at Deception, sending clouds of steam into the sky, blackening the snows with volcanic dusts. Scientists approached gingerly, for brief inspections only. They found mosses and lichens soon regenerating under the volcanic ashes, while the penguins, they reported, had blistered feet.

The birds of the Southern Ocean cannot afford to be too choosy about their breeding grounds. While they may spend months or even years in the air and on the water, no birds lay their eggs on the sea. All must come to land to breed. In the gusty expanses of the Southern Ocean there are only a few coasts offering suitable facilities, and these are the annual check-in points of more than 100 million birds.

'The rocks seemed covered with them as with a crust,' said Captain Cook when he sailed past an island shore in 1776.

Wherever there is a suitable cliff face, there are thousands of petrels and albatrosses going to and fro. Precipices are noisy with birds occupying sheltered ledges, cavities and stony platforms.

Day and night there are birds moving about the islands. Ships anchored offshore in the dark try to keep their lights dimmed, for like moths, night-flying petrels are drawn irresistibly to light, and stunned birds often fall onto the decks.

On shore, extraordinary sounds come from beneath the earth – the smothered wails, shrieks and cries of burrowing petrels. Their nests so undermine the ground that it collapses beneath a heavy step.

But it is the penguin colonies that visitors remember. King penguins, chinstrap, Adélie, macaroni and rockhopper penguins – they breed in colonies that can exceed 100 000 birds, while gatherings of tens of thousands of birds are not uncommon.

'The stench is overpowering,' said Moseley when he encountered his first rockhopper penguins. 'The yelling of the birds perfectly terrifying. I can call it nothing else. The nests are placed so thickly that you cannot help treading on eggs and young birds at almost every step. A parent bird sits on each nest with its sharp beak erect and open ready to bite, yelling savagely "caa caa urr urr" and its red eye gleaming and its plume at half cock quivering with rage. No sooner are your legs within reach than they are furiously bitten, often by two or three birds at once. At first you try to avoid the nests but soon find it impossible. Then maddened almost by pain, stench and noise, you have recourse to brutality. *Thump, thump, thump* goes your stick and at each blow down goes a bird. *Thud, thud, thud* you hear from the men behind you as they kick the birds right and left off the nests, and you go on a bit, thump and smash, whack, thud, "caa caa urr urr" and the path behind you is strewed with the dead, dying and bleeding.

'Of course it is horribly cruel to kill whole families of innocent birds,' he admitted, 'but it is absolutely necessary. One must cross the rookeries in order to explore the island at all and collect the plants and survey the coast at height.'

The teeming penguins provide eggs, chicks and carcasses for a crowd of scavenging hangers-on. Sheathbills loiter about the rookeries, birds that distract adult penguins feeding their chicks, making them drop the food and then pouncing on the spilt meals.

Giant petrels are scavengers at penguin rookeries, too, although these birds can barely walk on land, and lurch awkwardly with outstretched wings to peck at carcasses.

Directly or indirectly, however, all of these birds are dependent on the sea. Recently, scientists have turned to studying the roles of seabirds as transporters of nutrients from the sea to the land, and ultimately back to the sea. Marion Island is the focus of these studies. Marion is a 300 square kilometre, volcanic dome with snow-capped highlands and a wind desert of black lava. The island has poorly developed soils which are deficient in mineral elements. But on the coast there is a wet, green, lowland strip where more than two million birds gather every year.

For much of the year these birds scatter to forage widely over the Southern Ocean. But when breeding they are crammed together on the island and concentrate their hunt for food in nearby waters.

At the end of each summer the surface-nesting birds on Marion Island have contributed 32 000 tonnes of fresh guano, 500 tonnes of feathers, 350 tonnes of dead birds and 200 tonnes of eggs. Converted to kilojoules, in eggs alone the birds have brought enough energy to the island to drive a small car eight times round the world, or enough energy to sustain an active man for 300 years. And these calculations take no account of the input of hundreds of thousands of night-flying birds which nest in subterranean burrows on Marion, for studying birds underground and in darkness presents problems.

The seabirds have a profound influence on the island's vegetation. Guano and other fertilizing products promote luxuriant growth of plants. On the other hand, the steady tramp of flat-footed penguins kills vegetation along regular routes, leading to gully erosion. And when half a million of these birds are gathered in one rookery, they erode the soil to bare rock. Penguins have lowered the soft peats in some places by two metres. After even a light shower, the sea around Marion Island's rookeries is stained with slush and eroding soil. Yet this soil erosion is part of the cycle which returns minerals to the sea, enriching the inshore waters.

Men who dive beneath the waves close to the islands are always amazed at the splendour of the underwater life they find there. Tiny yellow crustaceans crawl about on mauve sponges. The tentacles of pink and orange sea anemones hang from crevices. In the shelter of boulders there are delicate hydroids, and dense aggregations of polychaete worms. Starfish are common and beautiful comb jellies drift through the dark water. Kelp and other seaweeds grow luxuriantly.

These plants and animals gain from the eroding island – and in turn help to provide an abundance of food for birds and mammals which feed close to the coast, sheltered by the swirling fronds of kelp which subdue the surf.

The Southern Ocean islands generally support insufficient insect or plant food to keep birds independent of the sea, even for part of the year, so it is not surprising that where birds cannot find enough to eat, man has had difficulties too. Over the years he has brought his animal food – sheep, goats, cattle, pigs, rabbits and reindeer – with him to the islands and the effects have often been devastating to the islands' indigenous plants and animals.

Sealers were not renowned for their foresight, yet in 1874 they told Moseley 'it would not be well to introduce pigs to the southern islands as they would destroy the birds, the main support of chance castaway mariners'.

Rats and mice reached island shores in sealers' boats – and cats were landed to control them. In 1949 a South African meteorological team took four cats to Marion Island; today an estimated 2 000 cats run wild, killing perhaps 600 000 defenceless ground-nesting birds every year.

Many islands have been changed since man paid his first visits only 200 years ago. A few land birds have become extinct. Rusting boilers and old trypots stand on the beaches as monuments to the days when penguins and elephant seals were slaughtered for oil. At derelict whaling stations the wind rattles and bangs among broken timbers and twisted iron.

There are some islands, however, so remote, their shores so inaccessible, that they still provide rare examples of undisturbed ecosystems. Sir Joseph Hooker saw their significance 130 years ago. On the islands of the Southern Ocean, he said, man could acquire 'knowledge of the great laws according to which plants are distributed over the globe'.

The basic natural rules attending environmental change are most easily found in simple, unspoilt communities. The Antarctic islands are field laboratories where natural evolution can be seen at work.

50 52
51

7 The Long Night

By April the mass evacuation is under way – birds have left, whales have gone. Ships are withdrawing, heading north. Whenever there is a lull in the wind, a film of ice slips over the water. The summer brightness sputters out.

As darker shadows muffle the sea, there is a stir of change on the ocean bed. Hydroids bare their arms like winter orchards, corals shrivel and sea cucumbers retract their tentacles and slump together, resting. Plankton sinks into deeper waters. Hordes of tiny grazing animals no bigger than fleas take up residence in their winter quarters – a warm current more than 200 metres down. Some have stored fats to see them through the darkness; others may switch to scavenge off the dead.

The winter ocean is a place of famine, a watery dungeon locked in rigid walls of ice. Sometimes the season of imprisonment lasts only 70 days – sometimes 270 and, in places like the Weddell and Ross seas, freezing conditions may last all year round. The ice is variable from one winter to the next, and the creatures of the sea have to be adaptable to survive its erratic shifts. If the ice is thin, the moon seeps through to the underlying waters, touching the fishes that nuzzle in glassy caverns. But when the cover of ice is persistent, the sea flows in gloom for the entire Antarctic night.

During cold spells ice forms like a white growth on the sea bed, even as far as 30 metres down. Snapped loose by a current this anchor ice will rise to the surface carrying sponges, starfish and algae embedded in its frozen chunks. For many living things within this dark, cold ocean, the touch of ice is the touch of death.

Some Antarctic fishes carry their own anti-freeze in their blood. This curious substance prevents ice crystals forming in their tissues at the very lowest temperatures reached by the sea, and so they can rest against icy walls, freeze-proof. Other fishes have to cower into the dinginess of ice-free deep waters, for although they can supercool their tissues, they freeze before the water does. If they remain at depths of about 500 metres they stay out of danger, but the instant an ice crystal grazes their skin, their body fluids freeze. Hauled up on a line they become hardened corpses at the very moment they reach the ice-misted surface layers of the sea.

Nearshore limpets fight the ice by oozing mucous onto their shells so that even if they are glued fast within a sheet of ice, the slimy coating on their shells prevents the ice penetrating their tissues.

Sea snails in the intertidal zone have a more mysterious defence – they have a knack of freezing their body water extracellularly. Although this distorts the cell membranes so severely that it seems impossible they will ever function again – with the thaw, the snails 'melt', and they are soon crawling about, undamaged by refrigeration.

On land, Antarctica's tiny land animals fall asleep or die. Fleas, missing their chance of a ride on a bird, overwinter as eggs in the debris of empty nests. In mossbanks, under rocks, colonies of springtails hibernate together – as many as 800 of these primitive insects lying under a single stone. When the temperature drops below a certain point, they fall into a trance, whatever stage they have reached, whatever they are doing. At a flicker of warmth, however, they revive to pick up where they left off, to feed, to mate, to lay eggs. Some springtails have to cram it all into only 57 days a year – for 308 they are comatose with cold. Although these wingless insects are able to withstand temperatures down to about −50 °C, one chillier hour is enough to kill them. Surviving the Antarctic winter is always a matter of chance.

Snowdrifts bury the mosses, and these plants are able to remain covered for more than a year, sheltered but lightless. Lichens also disappear beneath the snow, although many have no protection for they grow on exposed rocks facing the black night gales. Cold does not kill them, nor darkness – perhaps not even time, for these dry slivers of colour on polar rocks are among the oldest living things on earth.

They can survive almost anything. Tested in the laboratory, the lichens go on living when given frost treatments dropping to −198 °C. Kept in museum cases for 15 years, they revive when watered. Their gnarled forms tolerate the sharp stab of swelling ice so that even with 90 per cent of their moisture frozen, they keep their vitality. Only the lichens meet the Antarctic winter head on. Lichens and emperor penguins. For as life flies out, swims off, retreats from the winter darkness, the emperor penguins march in.

They march in single file, tall birds with little feet that squeak on the polish of hardening sea ice. Their processions throw long shadows in the fading light as they tramp or toboggan 50 to 120 kilometres to their rookeries on frozen bays and backwaters. There are only about 30 colonies scattered around a coastline of about 30 000 kilometres – most on ice as stiff as concrete that lies in the shelter of icebergs, islands, cliffs or steep hills.

Here in the deepening twilight these large birds assemble for calm and dignified courtship. With musical cadences they seek out their partners, responding eagerly to a familiar voice in the crowd. But there are no vulgar displays of love-making, no shrieks of affection – the emperors are going to need all their energies for the winter ahead, so the paired birds just bow and call solemnly together.

They make no moves to build nests, but stand about on the ice expectantly while the sun disappears and the long night sets in. Then, in the gloom, the first emperor eggs begin popping out, one to each couple, to be held on their feet. At almost one metre tall, the emperor is the giant of the penguin family – with proportionately the smallest feet. Little feet leave little room to rear a chick – and the emperor needs considerable skill to stay on balance, feet together, carrying a load, and walking, too. But if the bird's small feet seem poorly designed for chick-rearing, they cut down on heat loss. One need balances the other. The emperor's life is organised by compromise.

Within hours of laying her egg, the female passes the egg to her partner in an awkward toe-to-toe shuffle, both of them craning their necks down to watch it roll between them. Then the female waddles off to the sea for a two-month foraging period, while the male crouches on the ice with chilled feet, wearing the egg like a bedsock through blizzards and diving temperatures. Now and again he gulps at a mouthful of snow, but there is not a morsel of food on the dark ice of the rookery, and he has to endure a fast that turns him from a plump 40 kilogram bird to an emaciated 25 kilograms. In fact, counting courtship, brooding and moulting, the emperor fasts 145 days a year.

'Take it all in all I do not believe anybody on earth has a worse time than the Emperor Penguin,' said Apsley Cherry-Garrard, one of the three men who set off in the darkness of the 1911 Antarctic winter to find an emperor penguin rookery.

Ten years earlier, in 1901, a party of British explorers had discovered the first emperor breeding ground. They were picking their way across a 250-metre precipice at Cape Crozier when down below in a little bay they glimpsed tiny figures that could only be emperors. The birds had chosen an almost inaccessible spot, and the men needed ropes and axes for a two-hour climb across ridges and crevasses before they reached the bay to find 400 adult emperors, 30 living chicks and 80 dead ones. It was October – the beginning of spring – yet the eggs had already hatched. The emperors must lay their eggs in midwinter. It was incredible.

One of the men who swung down Cape Crozier's precipices searched among the birds for fresh eggs with special urgency. He was Edward (Bill) Wilson and he believed that this giant penguin was the most primitive bird alive. If he was right, the embryo would prove it. But although he ransacked the rookery, not a fresh egg was to be had.

It was of the 'greatest possible importance' that somebody obtain fresh eggs for study, he urged in a report on the penguin.

Ten years later Wilson was back in Antarctica, but even before he left he was determined to do the night journey to the emperor rookery. 'I'm not saying much about it – it might never come off,' he told Cherry-Garrard in a dingy London office months before the expedition departed.

But at the end of June 1911, Wilson, Cherry-Garrard and 'Birdie' Bowers stood on the ice, harnessed to two sledges piled high with sleeping bags and camping equipment, six weeks of provisions, and scientific gear for pickling and preserving. Their load weighed 342 kilograms. Cape Crozier lay 110 tortuous kilometres away through the midwinter darkness.

'It is midday but it is pitchy dark and it is not warm,' Cherry-Garrard wrote. 'What is this venture? Why is the embryo of the Emperor Penguin so important to science? And why should three sane and common-

sense explorers be sledging away on a winter's night to a Cape which has only been visited before in daylight, and then with great difficulty?

'It is because the Emperor Penguin is probably the most primitive bird in existence. . . The embryo shows the remains of the development of an animal in former ages and former states. It recapitulates its former lives. The embryo of an Emperor may prove the missing link between birds and the reptiles from which the birds have sprung. And so we started just after midwinter on the weirdest bird-nesting expedition that has ever been or ever will be.'

They pulled away from their expedition hut, into darkness and out of sight on what was to be called 'the worst journey in the world'.

'The horror of the next 19 days would have to be re-experienced to be appreciated,' said Cherry-Garrard, 'and anybody would be a fool who went again. It is not possible to describe it. The weeks which followed were comparative bliss, not because our conditions were better – they were far worse – but because we were callous. I, for one, had come to that point of suffering at which I did not really care if only I could die without much pain.

'They talk of the heroism of dying – they little know – it would be so easy to die, a dose of morphia, a friendly crevasse, and a blissful sleep. The trouble is to go on.'

Temperatures were seldom higher than −40 °C, once as low as −61 °C. But it was not the cold as much as the night itself. 'It is the darkness that did it. I don't believe minus seventy [−57 °C] temperatures would be bad in daylight. Not comparatively bad, when you could see where you were going, where you were stepping, where the sledge straps were, the cooker, the primus, the food. . .'

Sleep was almost impossible. The men became frostbitten *inside* their sleeping bags of heavy reindeer skin. These froze as hard as metal during the marches and it took three men to lift each bag 'which looked rather like a squashed coffin and was probably a good deal harder'.

'We could not burn our bags and we tried putting the lighted primus into them to thaw them out, but this was not very successful. I do not believe any man, however sick he is, has a much worse time than we had in those bags, shaking with cold until our backs would almost break. The day's march was bliss compared to the night's rest and both were awful.'

Seven hours in the sleeping bags was compulsory, and eight hours were spent on the march. Routine camp work took the other nine. In the cold and the dark even small tasks were slow and fumbled. 'It took two men to get one man into his harness, and it was all they could do for the canvas was frozen and our clothes were frozen and sometimes not even two men could bend them into the required shape.'

Entering the daily log became an ordeal because the men's breath formed a sheet of ice over the page which their pencils could not penetrate. Day and night were similar, so that it made little difference whether they started to march at noon or midnight, and they did both. Their feet grew numb with frostbite, even on the move, and always when they halted they kicked the toes of one boot against the heels of the other, trying to knock life into their feet.

There was moonlight when they reached Cape Crozier at last and set up camp where there was a smudge of bare rock and gravel. They built an igloo-like shelter 243 metres above the rookery. Above them was Mount Terror, an extinct volcano, while below were slopes so windswept that the men needed crampons to cling to the surface and not be blown away.

'The view was magnificent,' said Cherry-Garrard, 'and I got my spectacles out and cleared the ice away time after time to look . . . over all the grey limitless Barrier seemed to cast a spell of cold immensity, vague, ponderous, a breeding place of wind and drift and darkness. God! What a place!'

The moonlight did not last long, and the wind harried the men as they climbed down towards the penguins for the first time. They were soon in trouble, blundering into crevasses in the dark, falling, sightless, down slopes of snow.

'And then we heard the Emperors calling. Their cries came to us from the sea ice which we could not see. They came echoing back from the cliffs as we stood helpless and tantalised. We listened and realised that there was nothing for it but to return, for the little light which now came in the middle of the day was going fast and to be caught in absolute darkness was a horrible idea.' They barely followed their own tracks back to the tent.

The next day they struggled to fit a canvas roof to the rough walls of the igloo, weighting the roof with blocks of snow. Then they made another attempt to reach the penguins. 'We straddled along the top of a snow ridge with a razor-backed edge, balancing the sledge between us as we wriggled; on our right was a drop of great depth with crevasses at the bottom, on our left was a smaller drop also crevassed. We crawled along and I can tell you it was exciting work in the more than half darkness.'

They hung on with their axes, cut footholds, dropped and scrambled and crawled again. And then, when it seemed they were there, they came up against a wall of ice they could never cross.

'We seemed to be stopped when Bill found a black hole, something like a fox's earth, disappearing into the bowels of the ice. We looked at it. "Well, here goes," he said and put his head in and disappeared. Bowers likewise. It was a longish way but quite possible to wriggle along, and presently I found myself looking out of the other side with a deep gully below me. We cut some 15 steps to get out of that hole.'

But they were down. They had made it.

'We saw the Emperors standing all together huddled under the Barrier cliff . . . the little light was going fast; we were much more excited about the approach of complete darkness and the look of the wind in the south than we were about our triumph. After indescribable effort and hardship we were witnessing a marvel of the natural world, and we were the first men and the only men who had ever done so; we had within our grasp material which might prove of the utmost importance to science; we were turning theories into facts with every observation we made – and we had but a moment to give.

'The disturbed Emperors made a tremendous row trumpeting with their curious metallic voices. There was no doubt they had eggs, for they tried to shuffle along the ground without losing them off their feet. But when they were hustled a good many eggs dropped and were left lying on the ice and some of these were quickly picked up by eggless Emperors who had probably been waiting a long time for the opportunity.'

Wilson and Bowers collected five eggs in their fur mitts, handed them up to Cherry-Garrard, and tried to hurry in the bad light . . . as much as they could hurry feeling in the dark for the footholds they had cut earlier, pulling each other up on ropes, treading warily over crevasses. By the time they got back, two of the five eggs were smashed.

'Things must improve,' Wilson said as they banged at their frozen sleeping bags that night, trying to force an entrance for their weary bodies. The men were weakening. The sleepless hours had taken their toll. They had not yet done what they hoped to do – but they had found a way to the penguins and it would be easy to find the way back.

'I do not know what time it was when I woke up,' said Cherry-Garrard. 'It was calm with that absolute silence that can be so soothing or so terrible. . . Then there was a sob of the wind and all was still again. Ten minutes and it was blowing as though the world was having a fit of hysterics. The earth was torn in pieces; the indescribable roar and fury of it all cannot be imagined. Solid walls of black snow flowed past us and tried to hurl us down the slope.'

The tent was blown away. Without its covering they would never manage the 110-kilometre journey back to base. This, they realized, must be the end. For 36 hours after the tent had gone they lay in their sleeping bags unable to light the cooker, unable to move, unable to hear each other speak. The roof of the igloo heaved and crashed as drift spouted inside and covered them.

'The tension became wellnigh unendurable; the waiting in that welter of noise was maddening. Minute after minute. Hour after hour. . .' Then the igloo roof went too and the men could only roll over in their bags, heads against the ground, waiting to die.

But after two days and two nights the wind dropped and they crawled out into the darkness to grope in the snow for their tent. They knew the search was futile, but it gave them something to do. Then down the mountainside came a shout from Bowers. The tent had been found – and miraculously it was still intact.

'This was our salvation,' said Cherry-Garrard. They lifted the canvas and its frame, heavy with encrusting ice, and had no sooner got it up again when another gale began to blow, pinning them down for another 36 hours. Then they abandoned the emperor penguins to their storm-ridden, frozen rookery and tried to make the journey back through the darkness to their base.

'The horrors of that return journey are blurred to my memory,' said Cherry-Garrard, 'and I know they were blurred to my body at the time. I think this applies to all of us for we were much weakened and callous. The day we got down to the penguins I had not cared whether I fell into a crevasse or not. We had been through a great deal since then. I know that we slept on the march for I woke up when I bumped against Birdie, and Birdie woke when he bumped against me.

'Antarctic exploration is seldom as bad as you

93

54 55
56

8   The Bird that made the Breeze to Blow

Two boys were walking on a west Australian beach in 1887 when they found a dead albatross lying on the sand. Around the bird's neck was a rough metal collar on which a message had been punched with a nail: *13 naufragés sont refugiés sur les îles Crozets 4 août 1887*. (13 sailors are wrecked on Crozet islands, 4 August 1887.) It was then September 18. The bird had travelled 4 840 kilometres in 45 days.

Unfortunately the rescue was not as swift as the bird. After the alarm had been given, it was more than three months before a French warship arrived at the Crozets to look for the castaways. All they found was an empty hut on Hog's Island, and a letter from Captain Majou of the ill-fated ship *Tamaris* which had been wrecked in March that year. The crew had managed to reach land in two small boats and they had kept alive on a cache of food left by another ship many years before. Twelve days after the albatross had delivered their message, the food ran out and in desperation they left for another island. They were never heard of again.

Those shipwrecked sailors were not the first, nor the last, to try the wandering albatross as messenger, for this bird is the greatest of all ocean fliers and its journeys are almost legendary. In 10 months one ringed wanderer flew some 15 000 kilometres. Another travelled more than 5 600 kilometres in 12 days. Immature wanderers may circle the world for three years before making landfall.

'There is a sense in which the Wandering Albatross knew, long before we men, that the earth was a globe,' said American naturalist Louis J. Halle, 'for in their navigation they return to their nesting sites by continuing in the direction of their departure, making a circuit of the earth. Carried by the west wind like a fish in a stream, the albatross may, in the course of its life, circumnavigate the world again and again.'

If a wandering albatross lived 25 years it could travel a distance of four million kilometres before it died. However, some of these birds reach an age of 50 or more, so they can easily double that distance.

The wandering albatross is a master of wind. With wings that extend more than three metres – the greatest wingspan of any bird alive – it moves with effortless grace, gliding through latitudes where the air is seldom calm. The bird follows a regular pattern of flight, rising into the wind, coasting across it, dropping, banking to turn, rising into the wind once more. And all the time those long, slender wings barely flap. Slight adjustments at 'elbow' and 'wrist' are all that is necessary to keep the wanderer soaring through storm and fogbank, across the greatest expanse of ocean on earth.

Although albatrosses can be seen flocking together over feeding grounds, the wanderers are thinly spread across the Southern Ocean, and it has been estimated that each bird forages over 30 000 to 50 000 hectares of sea.

Yet even when visibility is poor, and gales are pounding heavy seas, the wanderers seem quickly aware of the presence of a ship, and sometimes they appear out of the storm like silent shadows to feed on the churned-up trail of organic debris left in a ship's wake. Just as the birds are able to detect ships from a distance, so they must read omens in the surface waters that tell them something of deeper happenings below. For food is not plentiful everywhere in the ocean, and while wandering albatrosses will scavenge on ships' refuse, croaking harshly as they compete with many other avian hangers-on, the major food of these birds is not refuse, but squids.

Fishermen would give a great deal to know how the albatrosses catch these squids, because they rarely do so and their fishing nets seldom come anywhere near these elusive animals. Squids are among the most extraordinary creatures of the ocean, ranging in size from small species only a few centimetres long to giants that grow to a length of several metres. Their mouths are encircled by 10 mobile, sucker-studded arms, and behind the arms is a pair of eyes, in structure, astonishingly like those of vertebrates. Squids have a highly-evolved nervous system. They are fast-swimming predators, capable of changing direction rapidly. Their reactions to disturbance are so fast, in fact, that they can avoid most nets.

Because they are specialists at the quick getaway, virtually nothing is known about their biology. However, they do make vertical migrations to the surface of the sea, usually at night, often from depths of more than 1 000 metres. The darkness must sparkle at their coming, for many species have an elaborately-developed complex of light organs. Whether the lights are used to aid the vision of the squids, to attract members of their own kind, as camouflage or to attract the fishes and crustaceans on which they prey, nobody knows for sure. However, the bioluminescence of many free-swimming, marine animals is directed mainly downwards, suggesting that it functions to obscure the animal's silhouette from below by closely matching the intensity of light from above. Hence, this bioluminescent counter-illumination appears to be a form of camouflage against predators from below rather than from above. The flashing brightness of squids makes them visible from above at night as they rise to the surface of the ocean, and perhaps this helps the albatrosses to find them.

But the albatrosses must rely on more than chance to catch their prey. The birds cannot just bob on the surface, with furled wings, hoping that out of the immensity of sea a squid will pop up close to them. Their hunting strategy is more efficient – but what is this strategy? What cues do the wanderers follow in their aerial searches? What images are imprinted on the birds to enable them to recognize hints of the presence of prey that are usually hidden deep under the waves? And how do the birds catch the many-armed animals that are too swift for man? Do the wanderers have preferences, or do they pounce on any squid available?

We know that wandering albatrosses feed mainly on about 10 species of squid, not because anyone has observed the birds on their dark hunts across water at night, but because remnants of their meals can be picked up on island shores in the breeding season. Squid beaks are almost indigestible, and they appear in the regurgitated casts of food remains around albatross nest sites, and are incorporated in the walls of nests and the surrounding soil. The beaks of some squids, in fact, have been the only clues available to the scientists who would like to learn more about these animals. Some species of squid are known only from their horny remains which sea birds have deposited on the islands – the whole living squid has never been seen.

While wandering albatrosses have provided invaluable information on squids, there is very little information on these great birds' lives during their months at sea, for little is known about the albatrosses until they touch down to breed on one of the tiny islands in the Southern Ocean.

This is where the sealers found them, dozing with their beaks under their scapular feathers, on raised nests in the grass. The birds stretched their necks to greet the intruders, gently snapping their bills, clop, clop, clop – but making no attempt to move. The wandering albatrosses had never known threats on land. In fact, they could never have grown to their great size and attendant clumsiness on land had there been large predators such as foxes on the islands. They had no defences against strangers, and simply turned their heads, mildly protesting with snapping bills.

'They will bite hold of a stick when it is pushed against their bills,' commented H. N. Moseley in 1879. 'They need a good deal of bullying with the stick before they stand up in the nest and let one see whether they have got an egg or not. The old birds never attempt to fly, although persistently ill-treated or driven heavily waddling over the ground. Very many were killed by the sailors that their wingbones might be taken out for pipe stems and their feet skinned to make tobacco pouches.'

Albatrosses relieved the monotony of Southern Ocean diets – both eggs and young being easy to collect and good to eat. The sailors who climbed among the tussocks after food obviously knew nothing of Samuel Coleridge's *Rime of the Ancient Mariner,* in which the luckless sailor's ship was becalmed because he killed an albatross, a bird believed to be responsible for the wind.

'Ah wretch, said they, the bird to slay that made the breeze to blow.'

But there is in fact no legend of the sea associating ill luck with the death of an albatross, and unchecked by the superstition of the poem, sealers, whalers and other visitors made meals of albatrosses on every island they found them.

The eggs they pulled from the nests were then boiled, sliced and served. These were single eggs laid once a year, and not replaced in the same year by the bird. With the egg gone, a generation went too.

59

60

The Bird that made the Breeze to Blow

Casually the men chopped and cleaned birds that were as old as they were. Some of the birds knocked off the nests were dark-plumaged 10-year-olds breeding for the first time. Others were snow-white, perhaps 50 years old or more, breeding for the last time. Some were birds that had been mating with the same partners for 25 years or longer.

When Australian explorer Douglas Mawson went ashore on Macquarie Island in 1911, he saw a solitary, young, wandering albatross. However, piles of bones in a cave have told of a time when albatrosses were more plentiful. The cave, obviously once the home of sealers or castaways, was discovered in 1949, its roof blackened with smoke, iron pegs driven into the walls. A big crack in the floor held the bones – almost exclusively the skulls of young wandering albatrosses – all that remained of long-ago meals.

Macquarie Island lies at the fringe of the breeding range of these birds, but there has been a gradual increase and recovery of the wanderer population on the island. Elsewhere there are larger, more stable populations and the total number of breeding birds in the Southern Ocean is estimated to be in the vicinity of 75 000.

No man in his own lifetime can complete a study of the life history of a bird that lives 50 to 80 years – perhaps even more. Not until we have continuous banding records for many more years will we be able to trace the fortunes of wandering albatrosses as they grow from chicks to maturity and, ultimately, senescence. At Macquarie, wanderer chicks have been banded for 24 years, and some birds have become familiar individuals to the researchers who watch over the nests. Birds that were born on the island many years ago regularly return to breed at their birthplace after ocean wanderings.

Because there have been so few wanderers at Macquarie, it has been possible to mark most of them as individuals and to record their life histories. This has been impossible at Bird Island, South Georgia, where in an eight-year period, 6 000 wanderers were banded and colour-marked.

High winds and a heavy swell make Bird Island almost inaccessible to sailors, and on its slopes some 1 500 pairs of wandering albatrosses sit out each summer, undisturbed. There are always some albatrosses on the green hills, but November is the month when the crowds gather. The oldest males are the first to thump down at the breeding grounds, staking out their claims, in sight of each other, but at least 30 metres apart in places. Wanderers must have an unobstructed field for landing and take-off.

While they await the arrival of the females, the males have work to do, repairing old nests, piling up untidy mounds of freshly-cut grass. And here they are joined by their mates of previous years. Next, the younger birds gather for a three-week courtship of song and dance. *Craaaaak!* sing the males. *Craaaaak Craaaaaak!* And then with puffed chests and much beak-rattling, they raise their wings and stamp their large, webbed feet in slow but noisy dances. Sometimes the female will sidestep, too, or waltz forward until couples are almost touching. Mating may take place at the end of one of these dances, but it does not necessarily happen. If the birds are an established pair who have mated before, their greetings are cursory, just enough to renew the old partnership and re-establish the importance of the nesting site. Then, having mated, they both return to sea to build up fat reserves for the tasks ahead.

When the female settles down to nest-building, she uses her hooked bill to cut grass and scrape mud for building a hummock that may stand a metre from the ground. It is midsummer by the time the wanderers nest, but they go about their work in an apparently leisurely way. No amount of rush will help them for they need a year to raise their offspring from an egg to an independent bird. Even if they started in early spring, they would still have to be there through the winter.

A single egg is laid – coarse-shelled and equivalent to six domestic fowl eggs. For the next 80 days the parents take turns incubating their precious investment. But although they care for it faithfully, wandering albatrosses are so clumsy on land that even old and experienced breeders sometimes crack their egg as they climb on the nest. Young birds and newly-established couples may break the egg within a few days of laying.

Once an egg has broken, the parent birds leave the island promptly. The egg is also abandoned if one of a pair fails to return to the nest. The extra months at sea will put them in condition to return to breed the following summer.

If an egg survives the first few days it has a good chance of hatching, and in autumn the albatross chick will begin to hammer on its shell. It needs a couple of days, however, to work itself free and scramble out to look at its home. For the next nine months the view will be the same.

Although it begins life on land, the young wandering albatross, like its parents, is really a creature of the sea, its survival linked to the rise and fall of the unseen squids in the deep ocean, far from the nest. During the breeding season, wanderers which have been accustomed to hunt over solitudes of 50 000 hectares, are concentrated together so that they have to share more restricted waters, not too far from the island shores. Nevertheless, it is likely that they range hundreds of kilometres each time they collect a meal for their offspring.

Albatross parents brood their youngster attentively, feeding it on regurgitated squids, krill and fish soup. Within 10 days the chick is the size of a farm hen. Within a month it is old enough to be left alone for the first time, gazing out on the world from an untidy, unhidden, unguarded nest. There are no predators to molest the chick – but should it be handled, the young bird will eject a stream of foul-smelling liquid from its beak.

Now winter is setting in, and the nesting grounds on Bird Island are virtually deserted. All the wanderers which failed to rear young, as well as the immature birds, have taken to the wind and headed for winter feeding grounds in warmer climates more than 10 000 kilometres away. Only parents with young overwinter. The fat, 'woolly' chicks sit on their nests, waiting for their next meal. The chick is fed on average every three days, which implies that each individual adult is away for six days or more at a time. The interval between feeds is an indication of the effort required of the parents to obtain enough food for themselves as well as their offspring.

When the winter snows begin to melt back, the young wanderer is heavier than its parents and is changing its woolly down for the dull black and white plumage of a juvenile. As its feathers grow it begins to exercise its wings, flapping about the nest site.

Most chicks have launched themselves on their first wind journey after the island slopes are again noisy with the arrival of wanderers that have been away all winter. At last the parent albatrosses are free of responsibilities. It is too late in the season for them to breed again – and physiologically they are in no state to do so. As they manoeuvre back into the air, these wandering albatrosses face a year-long holiday from domestic chores. Together? Or do the couple vacation alone? Whether they separate or stay together, however, the adult birds leave their island with a date to meet at the same place again next summer.

As for the juvenile – it moves downwind out across the ocean. For the next three years it will feel only the force of air on its wings and, under its breast, the rocking sea. Until instinct begins to call it back to its birthplace, the young bird never touches land.

Young wandering albatrosses begin to return to the breeding grounds at South Georgia when they are four years old. And no wonder they are clumsy when they alight on island soil, suddenly anchored to a hard surface after the lift and sway of air and water.

The young birds have changed their plumage in the time away. They will pass through several moults before attaining full adult plumage, becoming progressively lighter with age. The four-year-old adolescent is half light, half dark, and is easy to pick out among the other birds on the breeding grounds.

Craaaaak the young birds cry. *Craaaaak. Craaaak.* And they spread their wings and raise their beaks to heaven and shriek and jabber and dance heavily, snapping their beaks.

There are no hasty marriages in the albatross family. For four years young wanderers return to their birthplace to sing and dance and stamp and shriek in an elaborate ritual which brings the members of pairs together and helps them form pair bonds that will last a lifetime.

Year by year the performance of the immature birds improves. As they learn attachment to their island and their mate, so they come closer to breeding. When wanderers are six or seven years old they may produce a first egg. But breeding is a skill that develops slowly over the years. At first the newly-married often bungle it, and it is a long time before they have the same ability as older birds and rear the first fluffy chick of their own. The youngest known pair which has successfully raised a chick was 10 years old.

By banding birds, by recording dates of birth and departure, by watching nests and counting chicks, ornithologists know a little of the wandering albatross when it is ashore. But in the lifetime of one of these great birds, the shore is no more than a brief stop-over place. We know next to nothing of the about 90 per cent of the 50 years that the wandering albatross spends at sea. On land we can approach close enough to the wandering albatross to remove the egg from under its breast, but in the air it is beyond our reach.

9 Beaches of Bones

Adolf Hitler changed the fertility of Antarctic whales.

As his regiments began their march across Europe, whaling ships withdrew from the Southern Ocean, calling off the hunt for whales while men were hunting men instead.

It was the first time in more than 30 years that the whales had been left to themselves, puffing among the icebergs. And the change was quickly reflected in the reproductive pattern of the females.

Ever since whaling operations had been expanding and whale numbers declining, female blue and fin whales had shown signs of breeding at an earlier age. Scientists speculated that this was probably due to the results of heavy exploitation – leaving more food, less competition, among the whales.

When war broke out the whales had a chance to build up their numbers. There was less food, more competition, and female whales began breeding at a later age. But soon after peace returned and ships steamed back to the Southern Ocean to resume the hunt, female blues and fins switched back to the pre-war pattern.

The first peace-time whaling season, the summer of 1946-1947, was not considered a good year by the whalers, with a catch of 8 865 blue and 12 877 fin whales. By weight of flesh, however, that was roughly equivalent to 22 600 000 men – the number of soldiers of all nations that died in the Second World War.

There was a time when a million whales came to Antarctic waters every summer, and the thud and jar of their gathering stirred vibrations in the chasms of the sea. They came in protracted procession – first the blue whales, 200 000 solitary giants that heaved like earthquakes through the water, shooting columns of foggy breath into the leaden sky.

Behind them swam 400 000 fin whales, swift, gregarious companies, as pale as ghosts in the dark sea. Then came 100 000 humpbacks, travelling more slowly, boisterous whales that bucked along the surface, throwing up storms of spray. And last of all, at the end of the procession, came the smaller whales – 75 000 sei, clumped in schools, and about 140 000 minke whales that squeezed through openings in the pack, ducking under the ice-mantle, cracking holes with their snouts when they needed to blow.

And while they were apparently not part of the procession, there were other whale travellers in the Southern Ocean every summer. Killer whales cruised in lanes of broken ice, their little eyes glistening as they bobbed up to peer over the edge of floes, knocking the underside of the ice to topple seals into the water. There were also little beaked whales with elongated snouts, and southern right whales which preferred the ice-free waters north of a 60° south boundary line.

Sperm whales, too, normally never swam as far as the ice. They congregated around the Antarctic Convergence, 85 000 males with huge scarred foreheads, and, near their bellies, inscrutable eyes that reflected nothing of the complexity of the largest brain on earth. The sperm whales seemed to gather in herds, their behaviour tied as much to the phases of the moon as it was to the squids that drew them down 1 000 metres into the darkness of the deep ocean. For more than an hour at a time they could stay underwater, hunting squids.

Some of these elusive, jet-propelled squids glow red and purple, or flash luminous organs like fairy lights in their dim submarine canyons. Some squids have tentacles as thick as a man's arm, studded with suckers strengthened by tough, horny rings. Perhaps the scars the sperm whales carry are the results of tussles with these strange animals of the deeps, or perhaps they are inflicted when sperm whale fights sperm whale in contests that roll the waters of the seas.

No whale apparently has a more complicated social structure than the sperm. Females and young stay basking in tropical regions when the males make their annual jaunt to the Southern Ocean.

Other species of whale brought their families with them. When whale numbers were at their peak in midsummer, the Antarctic seas were crowded with family groups, with bulls and cows keeping company, with mothers chivvying infants.

The first explorers of the Southern Ocean found whales spouting all around them. Again and again jets of grey fog rose in the frosty air. Sometimes 200 whales were in sight at once, blowing leisurely, swimming towards the ship, beneath it, alongside it. Sometimes the whales were pre-occupied with feeding, sometimes they lay motionless at the surface, apparently asleep. There were evenings when they sported in large gatherings, leaping in unison, thrusting their wet bulk out of the water, crashing back in a wash of foam.

'A fresh source of national and individual wealth,' said Sir James Clark Ross in 1841 as he watched all those smooth shiny humps breaking the surface.

His wooden vessels were smaller than some of the blue whales that stretched out 30 metres, weighing perhaps 100 tonnes. The measurements were to come a long time later, of course, from carcasses on whalers' platforms. All that could be seen of the sea giants, from the decks, however, were blurred shadows underwater, the wave of a fluke, a sliding back, the glimpse of a tail.

'But if I know not even the tail of this whale, how understand his head?' asked Herman Melville in *Moby Dick*. 'Much more, how comprehend his face when face he has none? Thou shalt see my back parts, my tail he seems to say, but my face shall not be seen. But I cannot completely make out his back parts; and hint what he will about his face, I say again he has no face.'

Among the icebergs the whales seem to be a mixed gathering, casually milling about. But there is not only order in their staggered migrations, there are clear divisions on the feeding grounds. There has to be some organization, for blues, fins, humpbacks, seis and minkes all feed on krill, the small shrimplike animals whose swarms sometimes colour the sea. Krill are not the only food of the whales – between them they swallow squids, fishes and copepods, too. However, krill are their staple diet.

The whales are sorted not only by species, but by size and class within a species. So the larger, older whales cruise in well ahead of younger animals, and while pregnant females arrive early, lactating females arrive late.

First to occupy the feeding grounds every year are the biggest blues, and they wallow along the edges of the retreating ice, straining krill through the plates of baleen that hang from their wide, apparently grinning, mouths. All winter the krill lie hidden under the pack ice, and when the ice melts back in spring, gradually exposing stocks of krill, the whale feeding grounds shift south. The blues steadily penetrate colder waters, slurping in the crustaceans, squirting sea-water out of their frayed baleen moustaches. Slurping and squirting, a blue whale is able to demolish up to four tonnes of food a day. While its eating habits may appear slovenly, they are certainly efficient. Ten tonnes of krill build one tonne of whale. In just 120 days the shrimp-like animals pack enough meat and blubber onto a whale frame to double the animal's weight, and keep it going for the rest of the year. When they move into warmer waters in winter, the whales feed at only a tenth of their summer rate – so their Antarctic meal has to provide the energy for a long winter migration, perhaps birth and lactation, and the return journey in spring.

Although the whales take similar food, each species has mouthparts to a different design – some with fine filters for small food organisms, others with coarser filters for larger portions – and this helps to reduce competition on the feeding grounds. So the blue whales tend to feed at high latitudes on first-year krill, 20 to 30 millimetres long. Fin whales feed mainly on second-year krill, 30 to 40 millimetres long. Minkes, on the other hand, take the daintier, 10 millimetre size.

There was nothing simple or haphazard about the annual gathering of whales in the Southern Ocean – complex and subtle interactions produced a system that shared the krill among a million hungry whales, as well as seals, penguins and many other krill-eaters. However, this orderly regulation was as hidden to the early whalers as the faces and minds of the whales they pursued.

The first Antarctic whaling expeditions were not successful.

For 200 years men had been hunting whales commercially in the northern hemisphere, one whale fishery after another booming and collapsing, and whaling fleets were being retired when news came of the large numbers of whales in the cold waters at the other end of the world.

However, the old-timers were equipped only for slow-moving whales – and whales that would float after death, not sink to the bottom of the sea. They could not keep pace with the fast-moving fins and blues they found among the floating ice of the south. The first

whaling station was established on the sub-Antarctic Auckland islands in the 1840's – but closed after two disastrous seasons.

But these were to be temporary setbacks. In 1865 a Norwegian, Svend Foyn, invented a deadly new gun that could fire an explosive-tipped harpoon to riddle the whale with shrapnel while making it fast to the harpoon line by means of heavy steel barbs. With the new gun, and the development of steam-powered ships, the whalers were in a position to catch the swiftest whales – later pumping the carcasses full of compressed air so they would stay afloat.

'It would never be allowed if it took place on land,' said biologist Sir Alister Hardy after watching a hunt from an Antarctic whaler in the early days of success. 'Think what an outcry there would be if we hunted elephants with explosive harpoons fired from cannon on a tank, and then played the wounded beasts on a line.'

After the original failures it was not easy to find backers for a whaling business in the Antarctic, despite the possibilities offered by the new technology. Captain C. A. Larsen saw the potential when he first sailed into the Southern Ocean in 1892, but it was years before he gathered support for a whaling venture.

'Why don't you take these whales at your doors – they are very big whales, and I see them in hundreds and thousands,' he asked an Argentinian audience at a banquet in 1903. This time he caught the attention of some Buenos Aires financiers. They asked for further information. In December 1904 the *Compania Argentina de Pesca* arrived in South Georgia to begin hunting whales with modern methods.

At first the whalers did not even have to go far out to sea. All the humpbacks they needed surged in the bays of South Georgia. These knobbled-headed whales tended to hug the coast, and they arched their backs and slapped their tails in rollicking below the island's snow-clad peaks. The humpbacks are the most 'playful' of all whales, and perhaps the most musical, but the men who hunted them knew nothing of the haunting underwater songs that they sing on their migrations through tropical waters. The whalers saw nothing of the ponderous grace of the 33-tonne animals – they had eyes only for the tell-tale blows that rose like puffs of smoke around them.

The whales had no hiding place. Millions of years before, their ancestors had been four-legged, land-living carnivores, but although their forelimbs had changed into flippers and hind limbs had evolved to just nodules of bone, although their smooth bodies had become streamlined, perfectly adapted to life in the water – they never lost their lungs. They became creatures of the sea, but they needed to breathe air, and because of this the whalers had a target. A whale's blow could be seen at some distance.

That first season at South Georgia there was only one whale catcher – but it harvested about 100 whales. The hunters had few problems. The ship would glide up to a swimming whale and, as the animal surfaced, showing a patch of gleaming hide, the gun roared. There was a cloud of smoke, a muffled thud as the harpoon exploded, and the ship jerked at the recoil.

With the long, thick cable of the harpoon flying after it, the whale would dive and begin to run. Often a companion would run with it, trying to assist as the wounded animal struck the surface, blew, headed down, and rose again in streams of blood, desperately thrashing, dragging the ship across the sea. And the ship played the whale like a fish, letting it run, winding it in, feeling the cable slacken until at last the dying animal lay alongside, spouting a jet of crimson, its huge mouth open and closing, its flukes giving one last slap in the air.

Dead whales were stripped of their fibrous blubber and their whalebone, and then the white corpses were cast adrift to float with the tides. On island beaches jagged heaps of vertebrae, ribs and jawbones piled up, and when elephant seals clambered ashore, they had to heave themselves over the bones, draping their round frames awkwardly on the sharp edges of the skeletons.

The Buenos Aires financiers were well pleased with the first season, and the company paid a dividend of 70 per cent. No product in the world was more profitable than the Antarctic whale, not even diamonds or gold.

Within a decade, 19 whale catchers were busy around South Georgia and the stench of rotting flesh could be sniffed 10 kilometres to windward. Floating carcasses bobbed in island waters, each dead whale marked with a company flag, its gay colours fluttering in the breeze.

'It . . . almost reminds one of a holiday pleasure steamer with crowded decks,' said Alister Hardy, 'but its passengers are birds; they are mostly Cape pigeons pecking at the blubber like mad.'

How long could the whales last? The question was raised even before the bays emptied and the whalers

had to hunt farther afield, out in the swell of the open sea. They still needed a shore base, however. No matter where they found the whales, the ships still had to tow them back to the shelter of the harbours for chopping and boiling.

And this allowed for some control of the industry, for South Georgia belonged to the British and the British set a limit to the number of shore stations that could operate on the island. They limited licences. They limited the number of whale catchers that could be used. They ordered that no part of the whale's body be wasted. They banned the hunting of young whales, and mothers with calves. And they slapped a tax on whale oil.

Every year the catches of Antarctic whales went up, but nobody knew where the whales came from, or where they went every winter. Nobody knew how old they were, how fast they could breed. Nobody knew anything about their biology so how could laws be framed to prevent over-harvesting? The oil tax was to pay for a study of the lives of the great whales.

Before scientists could start work, however, the First World War broke out. It was to reverberate in the guts of Antarctic whales. Whale oil was used to produce nitro-glycerine, a vital ingredient in explosives. Whales were needed for the war effort, and for a time hunting restrictions were lifted. On the battlefields of Europe the flesh of men splattered under a rain of bombs, and in the Antarctic thousands of whales died.

Even while Britain was struggling with the war, however, there were men of imaginative vision concerning themselves with the fate of whales. A most unusual government committee was set up and its members began collecting evidence for a remarkable document that would outline all the existing knowledge about whales, the need to preserve stocks, and the areas of future research.

This careful preparation had results in the summer of 1925 when the *Discovery* sailed from Britain to Antarctic waters with a team of scientists charged with uncovering the secrets of the whales.

It was the start of a series of investigations that has, to date, already produced 36 volumes of research reports, with more still to come, and which has laid the foundation of our present knowledge of much of the Southern Ocean.

But even as the *Discovery* slipped her moorings, it was perhaps too late, for 1925 was a historic turning point in Antarctic whaling – the year when the new

pelagic floating factories began to operate. No longer did the whalers need to seek shelter on land – the new ships were specially built to allow the whales to be drawn up ramps to be cut up on deck. It meant the whalers did not have to pay the British rent, licence fees or tax. They were free to hunt whales anywhere in the Southern Ocean. The high seas were beyond the law.

But South Georgia's land stations did not immediately disappear, and when the siren summoned whalers on duty every morning, two scientists arrived on the whaling platform, too – Dr N. A. Mackintosh and Dr J. F. G. Wheeler. For the rest of the day they worked with the nauseating smell of death, in a butchery where the meat dwarfed the army of butchers.

The weight of a large blue whale about 30 metres long is equivalent to that of 1 500 men. Its skeleton is as long as two railway carriages. Its coiled intestines stretch about 300 metres. Its liver weighs a tonne; its tongue three tonnes. Within the cavern of its jaws several men can stand easily.

A sperm whale was treated separately from the other whales for its oil was spoilt if mixed, and its meat was unpalatable. It was beheaded for its wonder oil, and the fragrant curdles of spermaceti that it carried within its heavy brow.

Tearing muscles, popping tendons and cracking bones were the daily sounds of the whaling station. Winches wrenched fatty strips of blubber, saws lopped spines, hacked skulls. Everything was fed to the cookers: entrails, ribs, tails, flippers, brains. The whales emerged from the cauldrons and ovens as parcels of manure, stockfeed, petfood and as barrels of oil.

Thousands of barrels of oil for busy countries. Whalebone oil for margarine, soap, shoe polish, lipstick. Sperm oil – the magic oil, unlike any other in the world – for precision instruments, textile lubricants, leather dressing for hides, brushless shaving cream. Nothing was wasted but the whale itself, Peter Matthiessen observed of a whaling station.

While the blue and fin whales were being hooked out of the icy sea and squeezed into barrels of oil, while company books were recording the products and profits of the catch, Mackintosh and Wheeler were compiling pages of notes, charts, graphs. From measurements of the separate parts of the dead animal, they were building up clues to the living whole.

Sloshing in the stream and steam of blood and oil, and clambering among huge joints, they examined, measured and reported on 1 683 whales in their first two years.

Occasionally they had to duck as a whale foetus exploded from its mother's belly, a sticky bomb weighing a tonne or two, hurled across the whaling platform by the pressure of gases within the decomposing animal. More often they had to dig into the flesh in search of the ovaries and embryos that would enable them to plot the amazing growth rate of the whales. They discovered that a blue whale foetus grew from a pinhead to a seven-metre, three-tonne calf the size of an elephant in just 11 months. After its birth the massive infant put on 90 kilograms a day, doubling its length to 15 metres before it was weaned at seven months. A two-year-old blue was 22 metres long, and had put on 13 950 kilograms of flesh since birth.

'A record of body building in the animal kingdom,' commented one of the *Discovery* team.

The whale might be a body-building champion, but its numbers could not multiply rapidly. Female blue whales were more than five years old before they had their first calves – female fins were about eleven at sexual maturity. Or that was the position in the early years of scientific study. As the pressure of whaling increased, changes came to whale society – changes which the scientists detected, as always, from the bit parts of dead whales on whaling platforms.

Female blue and fin whales began to grow faster, precocious adolescent fins reaching sexual maturity at only six years old. But while they were maturing earlier, they were dying earlier, too. Smaller and smaller corpses were cut up by the whalers. A giant whale became a rare sight in the Antarctic.

Wheeler and Mackintosh spent their summers at South Georgia, their winters at a whaling station at Saldanha Bay, South Africa, and they soon guessed that some of the populations of whales they were working with were the same, for the gaps of information at one station were perfectly filled by the other. In short, it appeared that blue and fin whales spent only the summer months in the Antarctic, feeding, before migrating long distances from the icy Southern Ocean to mate and calve in warmer waters.

Yet their evidence was circumstantial. Direct proof had to wait for the results of a whale marking programme at sea.

In the days of open-boat whaling, whalers occasionally found old harpoons in the bodies of the whales they killed – evidence that the animal had been hunted before. In February 1910 a Japanese whaling captain, Tasuke Amano, began experimenting with marking whales at sea. The first 'marking rod' fired into a blue whale, off the coast of Japan, was recovered when the same whale was caught farther north more than two years later.

Before the *Discovery* left England, there were plans for a whale marking programme, and the *Discovery*'s men of science were sent out on target practice, firing markers at a large oil-cloth dummy, then at a stranded dead whale, and finally at a bit of blubber that was carted to a shooting range in North London on the back of a taxi.

But despite the target practice, whale marking was imperfect. The first metal arrows were fired in 1925, and whaling stations and factory ships around the world were asked to be on the look-out for them.

'Yet the years went by and none were returned,' said Alister Hardy. 'Clearly some factor had been overlooked.'

That factor was the ease with which a healthy whale rids itself of external parasites.

The whales were obviously rejecting the metal markers. A heavier, longer, stainless-steel tube was designed to bury itself in whale flesh and this was tried out in the summer of 1932-1933. Some markers were returned that season, from whales caught before they had migrated anywhere. By the time the Second World War broke out, 5 000 whales had been marked and the ocean pathways of the huge animals were being charted for the first time.

The darts proved that the whales were long-distance travellers, roaming vast regions. A female blue might swim more than 3 000 kilometres to calve in warm seas, returning 3 000 kilometres every spring to fatten up on Southern Ocean krill.

While each steel bullet could tell researchers where the whale had been marked, and where it had died, the scientists could only guess at the whale's voyages in between. The recovered marks gave no clue to the breeding hideaways of the deep ocean whales. Even today, after more than 6 600 fin and blue whales have been marked in the Antarctic, we do not know where all the blue and fin whales calve and mate, and whether they have specific 'grounds' for these activities.

The tagging programme had another limitation – success depended on the death of the whale. But then all whale research at the time was dependent on the dead animals brought in by whalers.

65

66

Scientists were well aware of the irony of their position. Before the whales reached the point of no return, they had to find the data to regulate the industry.

By the 1930's there were thousands of men hunting whales in the Southern Ocean – and about 20 men studying the animals. The industry tolerated the researchers, but when the scientists began urging that different quotas be set for different kinds of whales, the big companies simply ignored them.

Every year the killing was stepped up. Every year scientists made new breakthroughs. But 20 scientists could never begin to discover the complex re-adjustments of the marine ecosystem as the great whales were removed – nor could they use the knowledge they already had to put a brake on a get-rich-quick industry.

The summer of 1930-1931 marked the beginning of the end for the blue whales, the biggest animals that had ever lived on earth. Probably never again would there be a large migration of the blues, thousands upon thousands of them, travelling like cargo boats from the Atlantic, Pacific and Indian oceans. Their big tail flukes propelled them past the coasts of Africa, Australia and South America, following the old pathways that the blue whales had followed every summer for millions of years. They raised their broad, glossy backs among the icebergs, scooping krill in their grinning jaws, shooting rainbow columns of breath into the Antarctic sunlight. And at the end of that summer of 1930-1931 there were 30 000 blue whales less. It was a record catch – a record three million barrels of oil.

But it was oil nobody wanted. There was a world depression, the bottom fell out of the market, oil prices dropped by 70 per cent. In 1932 most of the whaling fleets stayed at home.

The whaling countries took fright. Britain and Norway had been doing most of the hunting, and now they met to agree to restrictions on Antarctic whales. The work of the *Discovery* scientists was used as a basis for rules governing the industry.

But the rules were not given a chance to work, for in 1934 Japanese ships appeared in the Southern Ocean for the first time. The Japanese had signed no agreements – and they had no intention of signing any agreements. They were there to take all the whales they could while there were still whales to be taken.

When nine nations signed an international agreement for regulation of whaling in 1937, Japan did not sign. Japan took a record catch of whales that season.

By then whalers did not really need scientists to warn them of trouble ahead – they had only to consult their own records. More whales were being killed every year, but they were smaller and smaller, and the effort of finding them made one whaling nation after another drop out of the business.

In 1949, the International Whaling Commission (IWC) came into being 'and gave Antarctic whaling its own polyglot bureacracy', said biologist Bernard Stonehouse. 'From 1949 the Commission faced the impossible task of controlling a powerful, profitable, highly capitalized, fiercely competitive, multi-national industry – one which had no intention of accepting controls other than on its own terms.'

The history of the IWC could be written in detail – the annual squabbles, ignored advice, critical delays, about-turns on quotas. But it is a tedious recitation and unnecessary, for graphs tell the story of the crashes of one species after another – and protection that came always too late.

In 1965, when there were so few blue whales left that it was no longer profitable to hunt them, their hunting was banned. More than 300 000 blues had been taken from the seas since Antarctic whaling started, but nobody had ever seen a blue whale mother nudge her newborn infant to the surface, teaching the floppy baby how to breathe. What family bonds existed? Where did blues travel, and why? How long did they live if they were not hunted? How did they behave when they were not afraid, when they were not being pursued? How did they find each other in the empty distances of the sea?

United States zoologists William C. Cummings and Paul O. Thomson once listened to the underwater voice of a blue whale off the coast of South America and measured its volume. It was, they said, a sound which could be detected for hundreds of kilometres – the most powerful sustained call of any living thing. But now that there are probably less than 10 000 blue whales left, does the call of one ever reach another? The blue was always a solitary animal. With so few of its own kind left, scattered in the ocean, will it be able to meet up to breed in numbers sufficient for a recovery?

In the summer of 1978-1979 one Japanese and two Russian factory ships with 34 whale catchers were still operating in the Southern Ocean. Although they had helicopters, spotter planes and sonar, they had to work hard for every whale they caught, and their main target was the minke, the whale that was once considered too small to hunt. Sperms and seis were protected in some areas – in others they were still a legal harvest. The fins, blues and humpbacks were protected totally – at least on paper.

Theoretically, most of the baleen whales of the Southern Ocean now have a chance to increase. However, even if the last whaler withdrew tomorrow, the future of the whales cannot be assured. There are indications that the relatively rapidly reproducing penguins and seals have grabbed some of the krill that was left uneaten when the whales declined. If this is so, the whales might be prevented from ever attaining their former abundance. And there are other factors to consider. Originally there were some 400 000 fin whales for 200 000 blues. What did the hunters do to this ratio? Is it being maintained as the damaged populations struggle to recover? Will the fins multiply at the expense of blue whales that may have dropped below the numbers required for a viable population?

There is another threat that might affect the recovery of whales in the Southern Ocean – the possibility of a large-scale fishery for krill.

'Until the arrival of *Homo sapiens obliterans,* there seemed to be no top predator in the Antarctic ecosystem,' said scientist Joel Hedgpeth. 'Many large animals fed upon euphausiids, and apparently nothing fed upon the whale. Now man is proposing himself as the carnivore most deserving of levying upon the vast populations of krill. But man is not a whale, and if he attempts to insert himself into the system as the ecological replacement of the whale insofar as consumption of *Euphausia superba* is concerned, there will undoubtedly be some unanticipated effect upon the system. . .'

And undoubtedly an effect on the whales, too.

Will the fishermen leave enough krill to let the whales make a come-back? If there is to be a krill fishery as well as a whale fishery, what quantities of each resource can be taken simultaneously? Some scientists are suggesting that whale stocks should be given a chance to build up to a size where they can be safely harvested – and that the most efficient way to harvest krill is to harvest whales.

The story of the Antarctic whales is not yet over, but what the next episodes will be, nobody is able to predict. Today in different parts of the world men swim among whales, eavesdrop on their conversations with hydrophones, watch them from aeroplanes like peeping toms. New techniques are being developed for study – no longer is all research being conducted from the bloody decks of whalers.

Whatever the method of research, however, we must always be outsiders to much of the whale's world.

'Dissect him how I may then, I go but skin deep,' said Herman Melville. 'I know him not and never will.'

10 Rotten Luck, Rotten Teeth and Crabeaters

There are no valleys on earth stranger than the dry valleys of Antarctica. They lie on the outer margins of life, so forbidding that even the glaciers wither as they tip over the edge of the valley walls, their hanging streams shrivelled in the dry air.

There are three major valleys, Wright, Victoria and Taylor, each about 40 kilometres long and five kilometres wide. They cut across the snows of the Transantarctic Mountains, arid hollows where the ground is shrunken and cracked with cold. Under the sandblast of the wind, rocks have been shaped into weird forms. The atmosphere is so sterile that nothing rots, so dry that snowstorms vanish as they fall.

Yet life has been detected in these barren landscapes – the life of micro-organisms, of slimes, yeasts and bacteria which belong to the beginning – and perhaps the end – of evolution. This is a world so small we cannot grasp its scale – so small it is almost impossible to trace. Recently scientists found colonies of microbes living *inside* dry valley rocks. They have probably been there for 200 000 years, ever since the valleys became deserts. The microbes must have burrowed into the rocks through cracks and pores, gradually swelling outwards. They were only discovered when rocks were heated and the outer layers peeled away. And microbes were not the only things living below the surface – algae and fungi were found there with them.

Looking for life in the dry valleys is like looking for life on another planet. When the United States of America began preparations for rocket probes of Mars and Venus, a team was sent to the dry valleys to investigate methods of detecting life in conditions almost as hostile as outer space. There was no better study area for the team's purpose.

The dry valleys and their mountain divides extend over 4 000 square kilometres, one of the few regions in the continent not overwhelmed by sheets of ice. Why the valleys are so different, nobody knows. The only features that single them out from all the other valleys along the coast of Victoria Land are their dryness, and the splintered slopes that stay brown throughout the year.

It is odd to find seals among the dry gravels. Seals are creatures of the sea, and the sea is a long way away. Yet the carcasses of seals are scattered throughout the dry valleys. There are dozens and dozens of them, Weddells and crabeaters, even a leopard seal – immature animals less than a year old. Some have been reduced to wind-dissected fragments of tissue, others are quite fresh, with a distinct seal odour. Several animals were injured dragging themselves across the rough moraine for they have cuts on their abdomens, and the sand beneath them is stained with blood. They look as if they have died in the past few days – tests show they have been dead at least 100 years. Earlier arrivals have been aged at between 800 and 1 000 years.

The dry valleys have preserved the dead bodies like mummies, without signs of organic decay. Only the windblown sands eventually destroy the seals, eroding their hair, cracking their skin, breaking them apart.

What makes the seals wander so far off course into these dead ends? Poor vision? Weddell seals have eyes with the capacity to adjust the aperture of the pupil. Immersed in water, in the glassy darkness under the ice, the pupil is round, enabling the seals to see well over long distances. Out of the water, however, the pupil becomes a slit that reduces the light entering the eye, and the Weddell seal becomes a short-sighted creature that may even suffer snow-blindness. When Weddells travel overland, can they see where they are going? Or is a hump of ice nothing but a blur?

Crabeater seals probably stray from inexperience – and bad luck.

In early spring, the crabeaters pup well out on the pack ice. When the young animals are four or five months old, however, the crabeaters move to inshore waters to spend the summer along the coast. Biologist G. Caughley has suggested that when the seals disperse north again, there are occasionally young animals with 'their noses pointed in the wrong direction' and once they shuffle off, they keep going, flip-flopping on lonely journeys up ice cliffs, over glaciers, through mountain passes. Dead seals have been found 900 metres up in the mountains, as far as 60 kilometres from the sea.

The natural features of the land tend to funnel them towards the dry valleys, and once they leave the smoothness of the ice sheet to slither down the valley slopes, there is no way they can clamber out. They are trapped in a nightmare of sharp stones and parched bitterness. The position of the mummified seals suggests they are drawn to features that are familiar to them – water and ice. Carcasses cluster near the shrivelled tongues of glaciers, high up the valley walls. The dead animals lie around saline ponds, along the courses of ephemeral streams that rise from meltwater at the height of summer, and seals lie where they died on the shores of the dry valley lakes. Some lakes are frozen blocks of ice, without wetness; others are salt lakes with icy lids that never melt although they float on warm water. Lake Vanda is frozen to a depth of three or four metres, but the sun shining through the ice reaches the briny bottom waters, and 60 metres below the surface the temperature is 26 °C. Lake Vanda is the most spectacular, natural, solar-heated lake in the world – but it is not a habitat for seals.

Obviously, seals have been entering the dry valleys for thousands of years – and recent tracks show that there are still animals that take a wrong turning from the sea. But although the mummified carcasses are of great interest, they are no more than curiosities. The fate of these individual animals is unimportant to the total seal populations in the Antarctic region – the estimated 15 million crabeaters, 730 000 Weddells, 220 000 Ross seals, 220 000 leopard seals – and the 600 000 elephant seals and 350 000 fur seals that visit island shores.

That adds up to a lot of seals sharing the Southern Ocean. Yet each species has a niche of its own, reducing competition. In fact the Weddell, crabeater, Ross and leopard seals not only have their own niche – they each have exclusive species of sucking lice!

Man knows the Weddell seal best, for it hauls out on the fast ice close to the shores of Antarctica.'The Weddell seal can at a pinch provide not only meat to eat, fuel for your fire and oil for your lamp, but also leather for your finnesko and an antidote to scurvy,' remarked Apsley Cherry-Garrard. 'As he lies out on the sea ice, a great ungainly shape, nothing short of an actual prod will persuade him to take much notice of an Antarctic explorer. Even then he is as likely as not to yawn in your face and go to sleep again.'

Like sunflowers, basking Weddell seals orientate themselves to the sun. They sleep deeply, lying motionless so long that they melt an imprint of their bodies on the ice.

These sluggish black and silver seals tolerate the pokes and prods of onlookers – even when the animals may be in agonies of toothache. Older Weddells have a lot of toothache – in fact they often die from rotten teeth. It is the price of being sole occupants of the fast ice – the Weddell seals live in the fast ice, literally hanging by their teeth.

Now, there is a lot to be said for the fast ice if you are a Weddell seal. The pack is jerky, stopping and starting like a slow train, piling up in collisions, breaking apart. In contrast, the solid ice fastened to the shore is peaceful, comfortable and stable. There is no need for tiresome migrations. The hulking Weddells can be settled, all-the-year-round residents with an all-the-year-round food supply. And not a killer whale can get anywhere near the frozen shore.

If the Weddell seals have a problem, it is breathing space. Neither food, predators nor disease is as important in controlling their numbers as holes in the ice.

'Presumably the first seals to penetrate the fast ice did so from the pack ice,' says biologist Ian Stirling. 'Therein lay the turning point of the evolution of their behaviour, for thereafter the very existence of the seals from late fall to early spring became tied to a critical resource – self-maintained breathing holes.'

The ringed seals of the Arctic have heavy claws on their foreflippers to make their breathing holes in the ice. The Weddells have only their teeth.

Walking on the surface you can hear them grinding at their airholes, rasping at the ice edge, using their canines like circular saws. After about 10 years of this hard treatment, canines and incisors get chipped, broken and worn down to the gums. Some animals have abscesses deep enough to erode the bones of the jaw.

The Weddells might be better off if they had teeth like those of crocodiles, which are replaced periodically. But the Weddells have no spare teeth, and aching jaws must be a common symptom of their middle age.

Of course they only use their teeth if they have to. Wherever there are holes, cracks or stresses in the ice,

70

71

they find them. Marine biologists breaking holes through the surface ice in isolated areas are amazed at how often a seal will come swimming from below. The animals seem able to find the tiniest opening – and several will share the ventilation.

It would be as wrong to judge the Weddells by their corpulent indifference on the ice as it would be to judge mankind by the hours spent asleep in bed, for the Weddell seal is a nocturnal animal, its round, soft eyes sharpened by the dusk, its 370 kilogram body transformed underwater to a swift, lithe predator that can outdistance the fishes it chases in the dark sea. It has an acute sense of orientation, finding its way easily through the featureless horizons of the ocean.

'One of the most beautiful sights in the winter was to see the seals outlined in phosphorescent light, swimming and hunting in the dark water,' said Cherry-Garrard. It is a rare winter, however, when there is open water close to shore. Usually the platform of ice is solid and you only know the seals are there because their voices can be heard calling from hidden caverns.

In 1966, biologist Gerald Kooyman and colleagues began observations to find out what the seals did when they were underwater. First an ice-hole was blasted and sawn on an isolated part of the fast ice, away from other cracks or holes. A heated laboratory hut was placed over the hole – and then from elsewhere unwary seals were captured, loaded on a sled, and towed to the hut. They were fitted with depth recorders – and given their freedom. Usually the seals entered the ice hole right away, and began making short, shallow dives to familiarise themselves with their new surroundings. It soon became apparent that the stout, lazy Weddell seal of the surface ice was a master of the under-ice environment.

It could hold its breath 20, 40, even 70 minutes, and regularly dived from 180 to 360 metres when hunting fish. One Weddell seal was measured diving 600 metres below the surface.

The Weddell seals spend most of the winter under the ice, sheltering in the water from cold, storms and gales. Bulls patrol their underwater territories along the ice crack. They fight in the water, biting at their opponents' rear flippers and genitals. They copulate in the water, too, the bulls lying at a breathing hole, whistling and gurgling to entice a willing cow off the ice, away from her pup, for mating takes place about a month after the pups are born.

The cows begin to haul out on the surface ice when the weather grows brighter between September and November. Groups of expectant mothers gather around one hole – usually under the watchful eye of a bull.

It may be summer but air temperatures can go down to −60 °C, and the wind may be screaming past at 30 metres a second when the young seals plop from the warmth of the womb out onto the hard ice, the amniotic fluid freezing on their erect fur as they emerge into the world. There is little a Weddell mother can do to shelter her single newborn pup; she cannot carry it, or lift it up, so it begins life with the feel of the cold Antarctic ice under its 30-kilogram frame, relying on a layer of blubber to keep itself warm.

The mother offers little to her offspring except a rich supply of milk, and in 10 days the pup has doubled its weight. At about this time it enters the water, the mother swimming with it at first, helping it out of the water. At six months when the pup is weaned, it is a hefty 110-kilogram youngster well able to look after itself.

The Weddell seal was an essential source of food for early Antarctic expeditions. It was easy to kill as it lolled on the ice, digesting a heavy meal, offering no resistance to its attacker. Some of the men in Scott's party in 1910-1913 killed a Weddell seal with 36 fishes in its stomach 'not too far digested to be eatable. We never again found a seal with an eatable meal inside him, but we were always hoping to do so and a kill was always a gamble. Whenever a seal was sighted in future someone said: "Fish!" and there was always a scramble to search the beast first.'

Recently 36 men at a New Zealand base dined off an Antarctic cod that was taken from the mouth of a Weddell seal as it surfaced at its ice hole. No sooner had the seal's head come clear of the water, than an observant scientist dropped a hook into the cod's mouth and hung on tight. After a brief tussle he 'caught' a fish that weighed about 17 kilograms.

In the Antarctic, Weddell seals are the traditional, the cheapest and the best dog food. Men may turn up their noses at the black, highly-flavoured meat, but it keeps the sledge-pulling huskies in good condition throughout the winter months, and some bases have rows of seal carcasses laid out in the snow to provide frozen fresh meat for the dogs. Although the total number of Weddells killed for dog food in any area is trivial compared to the whole population, killings have dented local communities. Ian Stirling found that the harvest of Weddell seals at Scott Base, McMurdo Sound, between 1956 and 1960 was so heavy that it depressed the number of pups born in the area for several years, and only with new rules and restrictions has the local seal population slowly recovered.

If seal hunters do return to the Southern Ocean, they probably will be after crabeaters, not Weddells.

There are an estimated 15 million crabeaters – and the proposed annual crop is limited to a maximum of 175 000 animals a year. However, apart from an experimental harvest in 1964, they have not been cropped in the past and they are not being cropped now. There are two very simple reasons why.

Firstly, there may be a great many crabeaters – but there is no market yet for their pelts, flesh or fat. Secondly, they may be the most abundant seals in the world, but they live in the most inaccessible region: the Antarctic pack ice. Spread out over some four million square kilometres, they can be difficult to find.

In the winter darkness the crabeaters live on a floating homeland that shudders and jolts and clanks under them. But whatever the disadvantages of the shifting pack, it offers one great benefit to the crabeaters: their privacy is seldom invaded. Even prying scientists have had their ingenuity defeated by the pack.

Crabeaters are slender, sun-bleached animals – gypsy creatures with no fixed abode. During the breeding season they are found in pairs or in family groups of parents and pup, scattered here and there among the bumpy white mazes of ice. They do not gather in crowded rookeries. When the pack breaks up in summer, groups of 30 or 40 crabeaters may be seen basking together on a passing floe – but they are here today, gone tomorrow.

'They are not a promising subject for study,' biologists agreed when they first turned their attention to the seals in the 1960's. And while their studies of dead specimens have shed some light on the biology of these seals, the lifestyle of the crabeaters remains something of a mystery.

'Little is known about their breeding since it occurs in spring when the ice is at its maximum,' say research reports.

'After weaning pups *probably* disperse to form groups in the pack. . .'

'Their winter distribution is not known but *probably* occupies the fringe of the pack ice. . .'

'Crabeaters are *thought* to feed 11 months of the year. . .'

In 1964 a Russian research worker, G. A. Solyanik, reported, '. . . during fall great permanent aggregations of Crabeaters (up to 3 000 specimens in the field of vision) assembled on the edge of the pack ice. . .'

However, when a Norwegian ship, MV *Polarhov*, worked the pack ice on an exploratory sealing expedition that same year, it saw no signs of such tantalising groups. Because fur seals gather in crowds on their breeding beaches, their killing has presented relatively few problems. But finding crabeater seals in the pack, is slow, difficult and perhaps not economic. During the two-month trip of the MV *Polarhov*, 1 127 seals were killed; and the sealers discovered the many problems of working in the pack.

Winds compacted the ice, and without leads to follow, the ship could only cruise at the ice edge. For a period of 11 days it was trapped in the ice. When seals were found they were usually in ones or twos, lying on floes. Even with a helicopter assisting the ship, only 964 crabeaters were sighted over an area of 5 620 square kilometres. The men in the helicopter also saw what could not be seen from the ship – that the seals tended to concentrate up to nine kilometres away from open water.

Although this first sealing expedition into the Antarctic pack was disappointing as a profit-making venture, it raised an alarm that a seal rush might soon be on the way.

But sometime in 1961, somewhere in the tiptoe world of diplomacy, somebody had already started work anticipating the arrival of the sealers. Soon afterwards the Antarctic Treaty nations turned to their biologists for advice. If sealing started, they asked, how should the industry be regulated and what limit should be set on catches?

Eleven years later, in 1972, the Treaty nations signed a unique international agreement, *The Convention for the Conservation of Antarctic Seals*. And 17 years after the first moves behind the scenes, on 11 March 1978, the Convention came into force at last, ratified by seven countries. The Convention is an example of the slow progress of international agreements – 17 years is a long time to wait.

The agreement has flaws of course. If sealing started tomorrow and the sealers ignored the rules, to do what they liked, take what they could, there would be no law or police force to stop them. The controls listed in the Convention are voluntary – they cannot be enforced. However, the Convention is an attempt to

127

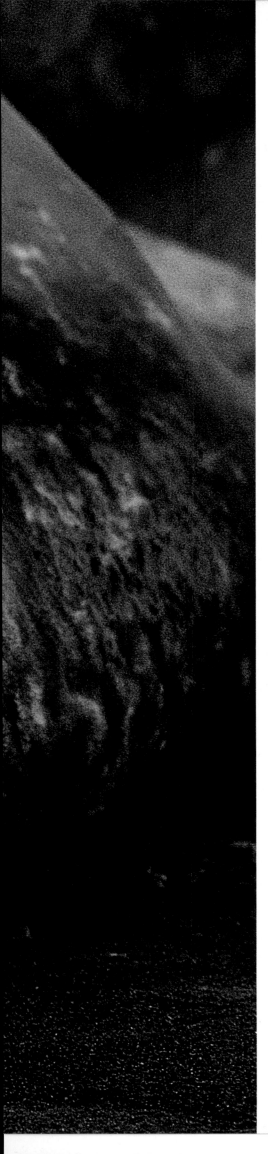

77 78
79

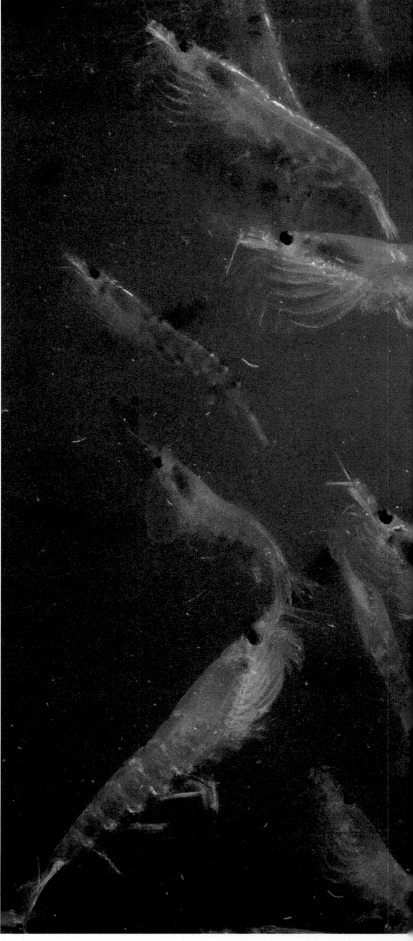

87 88

89

rotten. Even in storage, dry, sterilized or frozen, krill are an unstable commodity. Krill taste too strong – or too bland; develop a sharp cold-store flavour; easily turn rancid; produce a bitter after taste; have an unpleasant odour. Often the contents of the gut taint the meat and even colour it green.

Year by year ships trawling for krill in the Southern Ocean have carried on board more food scientists, food technologists and food processing engineers – all trying to make krill into tasty food for man. If their efforts have been costly, they are gradually seeing results in a variety of krill products. Good quality tail meats can now be produced – although they contain occasional eyeballs and shell fragments. The eyeballs also survive in krill mince, which is used for pie fillings, soups, mayonnaise and salads.

Several countries have turned krill into a coagulated paste, a pink to carrot-red curdled granular mass. The Russians sell their brand as *Pasta Okean* – bought by the catering trade for stuffed eggs and paté, and for enhancing the flavour of butter, cheese and vegetables. Chileans sell breaded krill sticks, the Norwegians feed frozen krill to stock.

Krill would be less of a problem if they were used as fish meal for stock feed. However, human foods have been the aim of most experimental work, because no other way can the krill industry be economically viable. There are serious doubts about the profits from krill. Who will buy krill? What will they pay for krill? Will the price cover the cost of sending ships 10 000 kilometres to remote and dangerous fishing grounds for a fishing season of three months a year? What will the ships do the rest of the year?

'The cost and earnings cannot yet be predicted with sufficient precision to satisfy administrators, bankers or entrepreneurs,' said a recent report produced for the Food and Agriculture Organisation (FAO) of the United Nations by G. O. Eddie.

Krill may be protein – but they are a novelty food. People do not have to have krill – they are going to have to be persuaded to need them. And, as the FAO report points out, krill have no advantages over any other seafood.

'For many years to come the raw material resource will greatly exceed the demand,' says Eddie. 'This will lead to a situation, unusual in commercial fisheries, where competition is not for the resource, but for the market.'

Krill products, he predicts, will be 'generally sophis-

ticated and costly . . . thus the utilization of the resource will tend to be limited initially to a few of the developed countries'. Eddie thinks, however, that 'increasing affluence', among other things, might step up the demand for krill in the future.

The affluent eat stuffed eggs and paté – not the poor. If krill are to reach the poor, krill foods will have to be subsidized.

And yet, from the earliest days of krill fishing, the bright crustaceans have been advertised as 'cheap protein for a hungry world'. It is a good slogan to muffle the critics of an embryo industry that is talking of harvesting a 'surplus' 100 million tonnes of krill a year.

The so-called surplus has been obtained by killing off the whales.

In 1900, before whaling ships began hunting in the Southern Ocean, it is likely that whales took 190 million tonnes of krill a year. Now there are so few whales left that they take only 43 million tonnes. Using simple arithmetic, theoretically, that leaves about 150 million tonnes of krill 'going to waste' – available for man.

Krill lie at the centre of a classic food web: diatoms-krill-whale. However, krill lie at the centre of other food webs, too. Krill cannot be considered in isolation. When the whales disappeared, the ocean must have made adjustments to restore its equilibrium. Any extra krill floating around could have been gobbled up by fishes, seals or birds. In fact there are signs that this has happened. Female crabeater seals are maturing earlier, while there has been something of a penguin population explosion. Along the Antarctic Peninsula, and on offshore island chains – the same areas where whales were concentrated in the past – penguins have extended their range, and numbers have increased dramatically. The birds are perhaps becoming overcrowded. On King George Island, in the South Shetlands, chinstrap penguins have been observed usurping the nests of Adélie penguins. The chinstraps approach nesting Adélies and go into the attack, pecking at their heads, striking blows with flippers, until the defeated Adélies relinquish their nests and the chinstraps take possession. Researchers believe the competition for nest sites is a phenomenon correlated with the increased numbers of birds – and the birds have apparently increased in response to an increase in the availability of krill.

Krill are the main food of both chinstrap and Adélie penguins. Ornithologists calculate how many krill a penguin has swallowed by picking krill eyeballs out of the mush in the bird's stomach. The indigestible eyeballs that give food processors so many headaches, provide zoologists with invaluable clues.

Stomach contents have been used to reach estimates of krill abundance. A large blue whale stomach can hold four tonnes of krill. Antarctic fishes have been found with 2 000 krill inside them, and at least 31 different species are known to feed on krill. One night in 1931, N. A. Mackintosh and Rolfe Gunther were on deck when they 'saw a bathypelagic fish with bright luminous organs feeding on a swarm of krill a few feet from the surface in calm weather'. As Mackintosh said, 'There may be other surprises in store.'

Squids are too elusive for the catching nets, but their beaks turn up in the stomachs of sperm whales and many birds, and biologists assume that they, too, feed on krill.

Intelligent guesses based on crude data provide an incomplete annual balance sheet for krill that looks something like this:
Taken by whales: 43 million tonnes
Taken by fishes: 60 million tonnes
Taken by birds: 40 million tonnes
Taken by seals: 80 million tonnes
Taken by squids: 100 million tonnes

Estimates change all the time as new information is acquired. However, even supposing these figures prove to be exact – vital information is missing from the budget: How many tonnes of krill live in the sea? The estimated total annual predations on krill do not correspond with the estimated total annual production. We have to know how much is available before we know how much we can take. Equally important – sufficient individuals must spawn to maintain numbers. But is there any way fishermen can retain a spawning stock when they do not even know how long the krill live?

This concern lies behind an unprecedented effort by SCAR and other international scientific committees to see that the living resources of the Southern Ocean are properly managed.

'We are mindful of the tragedies that have befallen the California sardines, the Peruvian anchovies and the Antarctic baleen whales,' they say, explaining that 'we do not have adequate information concerning the stocks of Southern Ocean resources. Despite past research activities we have only very rough estimates of krill stocks. We have virtually no estimates of the abundance and biomass of fish populations in the

Antarctic, and we know almost next to nothing about Antarctic squids. The problem is further complicated when we consider the structure of the Antarctic ecosystem and the complex interactions between seals, whales, sea birds, penguins and fishes, all competing for food which consists mainly of krill. And since krill is the key species of the Antarctic ecosystem, it is not difficult to visualise that its unwise exploitation could trigger disastrous change throughout that ecosystem.'

In August 1977 an international research programme was launched to gather the information needed for wise management of the Southern Ocean. It is called BIOMASS – Biological Investigation of Marine Antarctic Systems and Stocks. Using information gathered from ships, from shore stations and from satellites, the scientists hope to have results available by the mid-1980's. 'The studies have been drawn up so that sufficient information will be available before intensive exploitation of krill takes place,' says a BIOMASS document. And research will be done in close co-operation with ships experimentally trawling for krill.

In 1977-1978 eight nations were involved in krill fishing and research. Every summer, methods and catches are improving. Echo-sounders now locate the swarms deep under the broken ice. Catches of 300 tonnes a day are reported to be practicable. By the mid-1980's the fishermen could be taking at least a million tonnes of krill a year. If there is a surplus of 100 million tonnes, will one million really matter? There may be an answer by the mid-1980's. Too many unknown factors prevent an answer now. For example: Are there distinct races of krill? Do the swarms have different identities? Do they maintain themselves in fixed areas, never mixing with other populations?

If there are separate 'races', trawlers fishing continuously in one area could seriously damage that particular race – although the total catch might be small when measured against the harvest available from the wider ocean.

There is another factor to consider: While the ships appear to be fishing in a sea of plenty – that plenty is the key to the survival of many Antarctic animals which live by precision timing, by long famines and quick feasts.

Whales have to grab as much food as possible in the four months of summer. They need large swarms of krill close at hand when they are feeding – they need a sea of plenty. When swarms are scarce and they have to

winter, our knowledge of the Southern Ocean will be full of blank spaces.

The pack is one of the world's great hiding places. For part of each year 15 million crabeater seals go missing in this region. More than 200 000 leopard seals disappear with them. So do 220 000 Ross seals. Somewhere on the fringe of the pack, millions of Adélie penguins are thought to overwinter. Under the floating territory of ice most of the summer whaling grounds are tucked away. More important, the winter pack ice covers the krill.

Krill are the reason that the world may soon wake up to discover the frozen territory that often closes off a major portion of the Southern Ocean. And the interesting question that will then be asked is: Who owns the pack ice? Several nations are already standing by, waiting with their claims.

To understand the situation that is developing today we have to backtrack to the time when you raised a flag to own a bit of the Antarctic. Up with a flag – and the territory was yours.

It took South Africa just 21 minutes to claim Prince Edward Island, an uninhabited dot hidden in the fogs of the Southern Ocean. One day in the summer of 1947 a naval officer waded out of the sea, planted a flag on the shore, and splashed back, shivering, to a waiting dinghy. If the island's inhabitants objected to the take-over they showed no signs of it. The fat elephant seals slumped together, sleeping.

In case any queries were raised about that hasty flag, the South African navy was back at the island for a second flag-raising ceremony a few weeks later. This time it was a full dress affair. A bugle sounded. A guard presented arms. Officers stood at salute. Then everybody adjourned to a nearby cave to open a case of champagne. Toasts were drunk to the future of the territory – and with these formalities completed, the men rowed back to their ship and steamed home to South Africa. And still the fat elephant seals slumped together, sleeping.

Early explorers would have approved the manner of the Prince Edward annexation. After all, raising a flag was a serious affair, even when it took place in godforsaken wastes of snow and ice. Men polished their buttons and gravely read declarations of sovereignty before mixed crowds of penguins and seals. The flags might be torn away by the next wind – but they were the first labels on the south.

Captain Cook began the Antarctic flag-waving. In 1775 he hoisted Britain's colours below the glaciers of South Georgia. Up on the surrounding hills nesting birds were startled by the echoes of a gun salute. But they were not disturbed for long. Possession Bay, Cook named his landing place, as he sailed off leaving the birds in possession.

Jules-Sébastien-César Dumont D'Urville raised the French tricolour on an offshore island – but it did not stop him claiming the Antarctic mainland for France. James Clark Ross, too, had to make do with an offshore island, and his flag, too, claimed the interior, but for Britain.

Frederick Cook, the American on the *Belgica*, scoffed the flag-wavers for '. . . the first chart of the new country was quite good enough deed and title as the empty formality of pinning a bit of bunting on a temporary post and drinking the health of the royal ruler as is the custom of British explorers,' he said.

By 1939 most of the vast space of Antarctica had been snapped up. Nobody could say the continent was becoming crowded – there were only a few dozen visitors that year. However, some nasty squabbles were in the offing.

Norway claimed her share of Antarctica by making maps.

New Zealand's area was a gift from Britain.

Germany bombed the ice with metal swastikas.

Australia claimed the largest chunk – for after all, while others had been chasing fame and glory, Douglas Mawson had led Australian teams on surveys of uncharted regions.

When the Russians arrived to build their stations on Australian ice in 1956, Mawson was there to welcome them. The Soviet flag waved in the usual celebration, but the Russians were not picking a fight. They were just reminding the world that they had a right to be there. Had not their countryman, von Bellingshausen, sailed Antarctic waters 135 years earlier and been perhaps the first man to sight Antarctica? A sailing trip was as good as a flag. Anyway, the Russians insisted, *nobody* owned Antarctica. Firmly, but politely, the Australians disagreed. *They* were rightful landowners, but they were happy to have the Russians as guests and naturally offered them every hospitality.

By the mid-1950's it was confusing sorting out who had rights to what. The Americans had arrived – but they made no claims, they recognized no claims, and they built their stations on neutral territory, for about 15 per cent of Antarctica was land that nobody wanted.   153

A Little Too Much

While this region lay vacant, three nations tussled over the Antarctic Peninsula and its outlying islands. (For a long time even the name of the peninsula was disputed, it was to have several names – among others Graham Land and The Palmer Peninsula – before agreement was reached on its present title.)

Britain claimed her men had raised the first flags in 1775. 1775! snorted Argentina. Why, that region had been her inheritance since 1493, when a Pope had generously ordained that the world should be split equally between Portugal and Spain. Argentina, of course, was the direct descendant of Spain. . .

In some quarters there was derisive laughter, but Argentina had another claim. She was nearer to the Antarctic than any other nation. Quite right, said Chile – and promptly claimed the area on that basis, too.

In some quarters the laughter grew louder. Who had ever claimed a country by virtue of being close to it?

And Argentina still had a claim in reserve. She was the oldest, full-time resident nation, having occupied Laurie Island since 1904. Nobody argued about that – but why should Laurie Island give Argentina the whole Peninsula?

By the 1950's Argentina had bases all over the disputed region. So did Chile. So did Britain. The situation became very tense.

'Protest notes were exchanged like cards in a game of snap,' said Wally Herbert, a member of a British team stationed on the Peninsula at that time. 'Ships' commanders and base leaders were directed to act with extreme dignity and politeness to any foreigners who came into their respective territories, which, since they all overlapped, became a battleground for etiquette. Ships escorted each other up and down the coast like devout nuns. . .' Once shots were fired.

The Antarctic seemed set to become the scene of incessant, unresolved, dangerous bickering. And then a miracle took place: all claims were shelved for 30 years.

A room in Washington was the setting for the miracle. Outside there was pale winter sunshine and the settling lethargy of the end-of-the-year. The big moments of 1959 had already come and gone. There had been riots in Africa. A revolt in Iraq. Castro had taken Cuba. Queen Elizabeth was expecting a baby. Russia had sent a rocket round the moon. Nuclear tests had been suspended – but 'Ban the Bomb' marchers went on marching.

Antarctic Treaty sets up atom-free zone, newspapers reported on 1 December, 1959. It was difficult to obtain good newspaper copy from the Treaty. It had too many subtleties and complexities to explain easily to the man-in-the-street.

For weeks 12 nations had worked together on the wording of the Treaty. Seven had claims to land; five ignored these claims. With old disputes simmering among them it demanded cool heads, patience, and vision. Few of the men in that Washington room had ever been among the icebergs, but it did not matter. As mankind shares a common humanity, so mankind shares a common earth. Sometimes we are big enough to recognize this.

The text of the final document began: 'Recognizing that it is in the interests of all mankind that Antarctica shall continue forever to be used exclusively for peaceful purposes and shall not become the object of international discord. . .'

The Treaty nations had solved their own discord by agreeing to freeze all claims to land for 30 years. That disposed of a great deal of trouble and left them free to plan the last continent in a new way. The Antarctic Treaty (which was not ratified until 1961) promised:
* A ban on military activities
* Freedom of scientific investigation
* Free exchange of plans and personnel between all nations
* A ban on nuclear explosions and disposal of radioactive waste
* Complete freedom of access to the area south of latitude 60° south
* The conservation of living resources.

The world is familiar with paper promises, but this treaty has worked better than most. Today Antarctica is the only continent on earth that is not divided by border fences. Visitors need no passports to enter; they can come and go freely. There are still no capital cities, but there are more than 40 scientific stations, the largest of them McMurdo Station which can house more than 1 000 people.

The inhabitants of Antarctica are still scientists who seldom stay more than a year at a time, but they have built up remarkable traditions of co-operation. Americans work side-by-side with Russians. No matter the nationality, all scientists in Antarctica share friendships, share projects, share the results of experiments.

Antarctica may have no voting citizens, but there is a

'parliament' that runs its affairs, made up of representatives of the 12 nations that originally signed the Treaty: Argentina, Australia, Belgium, Chile, France, Japan, New Zealand, Norway, South Africa, the United Kingdom, the United States and the USSR. Poland is an additional member of the Treaty to which another six nations have acceded since 1961. It is likely that West Germany soon will become a full member of the Treaty.

Newcomers to the Treaty are welcome provided they stick to the rules and pay the rent – which is the cost of 'substantial scientific research'. Not all countries can afford it. In the remote regions of the south, where man exists much as he does on the moon, carrying his own life-support system with him, a station or an expedition can cost several million dollars a year.

The Treaty powers have their scientific advisors, the Scientific Committee on Antarctic Research, (SCAR), and together they have worked out rules to minimize the impact of man on a fragile environment. There are standing instructions for expeditions, rules on disposing of rubbish (you take batteries, rubber and plastics home with you).

Nature reserves have been proclaimed. All seals and birds which are killed must be reported. There is the Convention on Sealing. Plans are going forward to control the growing invasion of tourists. . .

But. . .

There are lots of buts, and they all go back to three subjects that were left unspoken at the Washington meeting: minerals, pack ice and the high seas.

'It was inevitable that those who negotiated the Antarctic Treaty should have hesitated to imperil such a frail alliance by raising prematurely some of the ultimate issues of a highly controversial nature,' said the late Brian Roberts, a man with the perspective that came from 40 years of involvement in Antarctic affairs, first as a zoologist, then as an official at the British Foreign Office. 'It was not that the negotiators failed to foresee these difficulties. It was rather that, while the whole situation remained so extremely delicate, it was essential to keep disputes between themselves to a minimum. If mineral exploitation had been pursued in Washington there would have been no Treaty.'

By 1973, however, the matter could no longer be ignored. That was the year *Glomar Challenger* struck ethane and methane gas in three of the four holes drilled in the Ross continental shelf. The United States

Geological Survey jumped to some questionable conclusions. In 1974, a report was published 'estimating' recoverable reserves of 45 billion barrels of oil and more than three trillion cubic metres of gas lay below the ice on the western continental shelf alone. This was equal to the total proven reserves of the United States.

The estimate was, in fact, meaningless, based on unproven information not yet available, but even while geologists were voicing these criticisms, news of the 'oil find' shot around the world. Oil-hungry nations swivelled their attention to the south. Oil companies began to make approaches for mineral rights in the ice-choked seas, and the rumours of oil were added onto rumours about huge riches of coal, iron and other minerals.

Early in 1977, SCAR set up a specialist committee to look into the potential and the problems. The committee reported as follows: *No mineral deposits which are likely to be of economic value in the foreseeable future are known in Antarctica.*

But until the big, multi-national companies have themselves come to grips with the resources, the problems and the costs, there will be continuous pressure for mining rights. And if nobody owns Antarctica – who has the power to grant prospecting rights?

While there may be no quick fortunes in the south for miners and oilmen, there is an estimated 10-billion-dollar industry waiting for anyone who starts a business towing icebergs. Indeed, the day may come when 500 million city-dwellers all over the world drink and wash in water from Antarctic ice.

'The idea of using Antarctic icebergs has been carefully researched and even tried in a small way,' reported the Antarctic specialist committee on mineral exploitation. 'Theoretically icebergs could be floated to any point accessible by a water route with depths of at least 200 metres. . . All the feasibility studies of the last few years have concluded that towing systems can be developed within the limits of present technology, and that water could be delivered to its destination at a fraction of the costs of alternative sources. There are indications that this might become a reality before the end of the century.'

While iceberg towing will only have small and local effects on the ocean environment, 'It is one of the few Antarctic developments which might possibly take place without raising problems of original ownership of the icebergs,' said Brian Roberts.

Icebergs may cause no controversy – but the same

155

cannot be said for the pack ice and the high seas. In Washington in 1959 these were both taboo subjects because they might bring into the open the real reason many countries were interested in the Antarctic.

It was not the land they wanted. The land was barren. But if they had a right to the land, they could claim territorial waters. The riches of Antarctica lie in the ocean.

In 1959, 37 900 whales were taken in the Southern Ocean. The whaling industry was booming and the whalers had a government of sorts – the International Whaling Commission. As the IWC was already ruling the Antarctic waves, how could the Treaty nations set themselves up as overlords of the same waters? No wonder that Washington room handled the matter by resorting to silence.

When the Treaty was announced, its gaps disguised the fact that the Treaty nations wanted to fish and hunt as they liked in the Southern Ocean. Their promises were for land, not for sea.

Inevitably, of course, their laws became ludicrous. So long as an Adélie penguin was sitting on its nest on land, it could not be killed, wounded, captured or molested. But it could be knocked off without a qualm if it was sitting on an ice floe. Mossbanks were protected, whales were not. . .

The legislators had much to learn, and the biologists would have to teach them. Antarctic biologists were long past the period of simply collecting specimens and describing what they collected. They knew that any study, organism by organism, population by population, has as much purpose as 'the molecule by molecule approach has for predicting the pounce of the tiger', as G. M. Woodwell put it. '. . . the basic unit for management of the earth's resources is not energy, fish, food, oil – but whole units, ecosystems, that function according to a set of discoverable laws, not according to the whim of exploiters.'

Biologists could not pretend the whale crash did not concern them, because it happened beyond the limits set by the Antarctic Treaty. Antarctic waters might be remote but they had been the scene of two classic examples of mismanagement – first the fur seals, then the whales.

'The difference between these two industries was that the former was conducted in ignorance,' said Martin Holdgate, 'whereas the whaling industry had the benefit of expert scientific and statistical advice based on many years of research, and chose to ignore it for short-term commercial reasons. There is a social lesson in this somewhere, for what good is it to pay scientists to study natural resources if their discoveries are not used to improve management?'

The biologists were determined history would not repeat itself. They were not diplomats trained to hold their tongues. 'We draw attention to the overfishing of lobster stocks in the area of Iles St Paul and Amsterdam,' they said in 1975.

Next they queried Russian fish catches around South Georgia and Kerguelen. 'Peak catches have been 400 000 tonnes in 1970 and 20 000 tonnes in 1971,' they said. 'While the available data do not allowed detailed assessment, the subsequent decline in catches suggest the stocks have been affected by the fishery.'

Even before the krill fishery began to loom over the south, the scientists' discoveries were pointing at a very disconcerting fact: Antarctic waters were *not* markedly more productive than any other ocean. The great fertility of the Southern Ocean was a myth.

It was an attractive myth, which probably had its roots in the days when early travellers like Joseph Hooker sailed among the icebergs marvelling at the numbers of whales, the seals and birds, and plankton so thick it discoloured the sea.

The myth was perpetuated by every summer visitor who saw flurries of prions obliterate the horizon, who came within earshot of hundreds of thousands of raucous penguins breeding together, or an island beach crowded with fur seals. It was easy to be fooled by such abundance.

However, as the large animals of the Antarctic experience extremes of feast and famine, so the whole biotic system has only a few months to concentrate the energy it needs to survive the long and difficult austral winter.

The Antarctic ecosystem is an ecosystem under stress, limited by a shortage of solar energy and heat. Those huge populations of Antarctic birds and mammals are not signs of great fertility – they are signs of a system that lacks energy, lacks complexity, lacks diversity. Such a system is vulnerable to interference.

'We are tempted by Antarctica's apparently large stocks of krill,' says biologist Ariel E. Lugo. 'We should remind ourselves that in the managing and harvesting populations, stocks are not as important as their rate of turnover. A similar mistake was made in managing tropical wet forests. The large biomass of tropical trees gave many the idea of huge profits through timber production. Yet each tree took many decades to grow. . . Excessive harvesting of the tropical wet forest resulted in its replacement by unproductive grassy systems and the loss of the magnificent rain forest. This can happen in Antarctica if we set quotas on krill and other living resources without knowing their rate of growth and regeneration, or without understanding their role in the ecosystem. If we harvest too much so that the stock can no longer survive the stresses of the Antarctic environment, the stocks will simply disappear, and so will dependent species, and our share as consumers.'

In the Antarctic region there is the paradox of life adapted to survive the most hostile environment in the world – yet sensitive to any disturbance. So a mossbank may endure the cold darkness of polar winters – but a bootmark in the moss may persist for many years. Trivial actions dent the future.

This is the lesson Antarctic biologists have been sharing with Antarctic diplomats. If there had been time, together they might have devised a wise and careful management plan for the Southern Ocean. If there had been time, a law for the sea might have emerged from the Antarctic. But by 1977 powerful forces were being exerted on the nations in the exclusive Antarctic 'club'. Before they were ready the Treaty nations were trapped by their own Washington evasions. They could no longer dodge controversy by silence. Whether they liked it or not the Antarctic was more than just an international laboratory. It was a fishing ground – and 144 nations might want a part of it, too.

In 1978 the Treaty nations began drafting a new Convention on the Living Resources of the Southern Ocean. The world has watched at a distance, suspicious of any wisdom offered by a group that might be serving its own interests, sharing out the krill among themselves.

The history of whaling in the Southern Ocean has shown that compromise among reasonable men is not sufficient to regulate an industry. 'We cannot operate as exploitation does, compromising something for us, something for them,' warns biologist Carleton Ray. 'There are no us and them – only we.'

Biological truth, unfortunately, tends to clash with political reality. The Treaty nations have made one deadline after another for finalizing the new convention. As time drags on there is speculation that the Treaty nations are quarrelling among themselves on who shares the spoils; that land claims are being taken out of cold storage in the bargaining for territorial waters.

There is still hope, however, that they will rise above the difficulties of the past to produce a second miracle – a convention that will conserve krill, that will recognize the many nations interested in fishing in Antarctic waters, and be recognized by them in turn.

But much more than questions of law and freedom hang over Antarctica and its cold seas. From the chill purity of the south polar ice cap, men are measuring the effects of events on the other side of the world. Are pollutants from the industries of the northern hemisphere warming the earth, melting the ice cap, raising the sea?

Antarctica may be unknown and remote to us, but it is not separate. The last continent is a testing-ground for our future.

Captions
to the
Colour Plates

1

1. Out of the heaving emptiness of the Southern Ocean, a light-mantled sooty albatross appears suddenly, gliding effortlessly above wind-torn swells. For the south-bound traveller, this albatross marks the threshold of Antarctica's stormy waters. It symbolises entry to a strange new world.

2

2. 'A large berg full of caves and crevasses on a bright day is a most beautiful and striking object,' wrote the naturalist H.N. Moseley in 1874. The colour, he said, was 'of the deepest and purest possible azure blue. None of our artists on board were able to approach a representation of its intensity.'
Tongues of water have hollowed a passage through this floating iceberg. Flying kelp gulls give some scale to a tunnel so high that a ship could pass through the opening, were it not for the icy white spire that blocks the way.

3   4

3. When the first ships thumped into the pack, penguins watched them from the ice. Men gathered at the rails to grin down on Antarctica's reception committees. 'They always come up at a trot when we sign to them,' said Edward Wilson in 1910, 'and you'll often see a group of explorers on the poop singing "for she has rings on her fingers and bells on her toes" and so on at the tops of our voices to an admiring group of Adélie penguins.'
Here chinstrap penguins gather on floating ice.

4. The earth's crust has dented under the mass of ice lying at the South Pole. If the ice melted tomorrow, coasts around the world would be submerged, men would have to take to the hills.
Although King George Island lies outside the Antarctic Circle – that line of latitude drawn around the globe at 66° 33′ South – it has a burden of ice which meets the sea in frozen precipices up to 100 metres high. Penguins make a nesting ground on an ice-free headland.

5

5. 'To visualise the Antarctic as a white land is a mistake, for not only is there much rock projecting wherever mountains or rocky capes of islands rise, but the snow seldom looks white. It is shaded with many colours, but chiefly with cobalt blue and rose madder and all the gradations of lilac and mauve . . . A white day is so rare that I have recollections of going out from the hut or the tent and being impressed by the fact that the snow really looked white.' *Apsley Cherry-Garrard, 1910–1912*

6. There is a gale warning in the wisps of snow flicked off the top of this iceberg afloat in the darkening currents of the Gerlache Strait. The mist and clouds of the advancing storm almost obscure the soaring pinnacles of the Antarctic Peninsula which rise more than 2 000 metres above the sea. Storms generated in Antarctica can travel as far as southern Africa. In fact the continent is 'the weather machine of the world', for the ice sheet dominates and controls patterns of global climate.

7. All summer the sea has been cluttered with ice and now, as winter closes in, the fragments begin to freeze together. Soon the continent will be unapproachable by ship. But conditions in Antarctica are seldom predictable. Some years the sea is free of ice for 40 weeks – other years only 10.

6 7

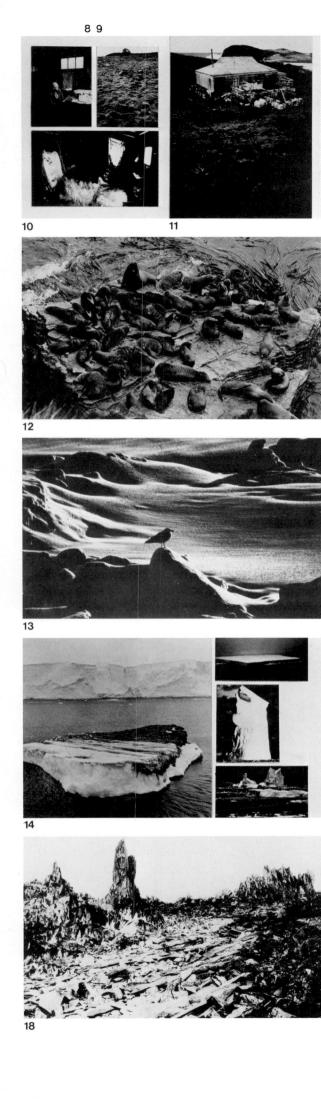

10   11

12

13

14

15
16
17

18

8. Lost in reflection, Sir Peter Scott sits at the chart table where his father, Captain R. F. Scott, planned his ill-fated trip to the South Pole in 1912. Scott never returned from that journey.

9. 'Avoid walking over mossbanks' is one of the rules for Antarctic tourists. Mosses and lichens are the most common plants on the ice-free areas of Antarctica. Only two species of flowering plants have been recorded on the continent, both in the northern half of the Antarctic Peninsula. However, moss tufts are slow-growing and the scars left by passersby can persist for decades. Close to the abandoned British Antarctic base on King George Island, bootmarks dent the moss.

10. The penguin eggs beneath the window were collected by Scott's men more than 60 years ago, but Antarctica's deep-freeze temperatures have preserved them. Slabs of seal meat have not decayed. Yesterday could be today were it not for the waiting ice beyond the window, ready to obliterate the present and the past.

11. 'Nothing is changed at all but the company,' said one of Ernest Shackleton's men revisiting his old base at Cape Royds, Ross Island, three years after Shackleton's 1907 – 1909 expedition. On a table, still fresh, were the remains of a lunch left uneaten when the men raced a blizzard to board their ship. Today caretakers from New Zealand repair and maintain this historic hut, still virtually unchanged since Shackleton's day.

12. A fur seal bull guards his territory as fronds of kelp swirl around a rocky platform off one of the Falkland Islands. On this spray-drenched outcrop, the females in his harem give birth, no longer harassed by the hunters who brought the southern fur seal to the verge of extinction in the eighteenth century. In 1784 alone, one vessel secured a cargo of 13 000 fur seal skins from the Falklands. However, the tally of animals lost must have been higher, for only adult seals were taken – the orphaned pups were left to starve.

13. Cold has turned the sea to stone and a layer of new snow softens the hard sheen of the ice; yet life has not deserted. A solitary kelp gull finds a perch on the rigid ocean.

14. For millions of years Antarctica was hidden behind her guardian ring of ice. But icebergs like this one eventually gave away her position. They were recorded by Jean Bouvet de Lozier in 1738 – 39 when searching for the fabled Southern Lands. Although he never sighted Antarctica, icebergs streaked with rock and sand convinced him land was not far off. Lines in the ice – like tree rings – denote its age. Each layer represents the annual accumulation of snow.

15. Floating sea ice has many origins. Flat-topped bergs like this one puzzled early travellers. Not until the continent's ice shelves were discovered did men realise that the tabular bergs had 'calved' from the edges of the massive, buoyant shelves. Some such slabs are up to 70 kilometres across.

16. Like a huge icecream cone, the pinnacle of a berg floats higher than a ship. Scientists are learning something of the movement of icebergs by tracking them by satellite. South of the Indian Ocean, icebergs have been timed travelling at an average speed of 15 kilometres a day. However, they have been known to race three times as fast.

17. Today Antarctica's ice provides a basking place for slumbering crabeater seals. Tomorrow the ice may provide drinking water for cities across the world. Feasibility studies indicate that there should be few problems in towing icebergs across the ocean to bring fresh water to arid lands. The first practical experiments are planned for the near future.

18. Cold has created this shattered desert near the Antarctic Peninsula – cold so severe that it has the power to crack and splinter rock, leaving a wasteland of sharp rubble. Towering behind the devastation is the distant peak of Mount Français on Anvers Island.

159

19

20 21

22

23

24   **25**

160

26

19. Antarctica was not always buried in ice, nor did it always sit at the South Pole. This fossil fern, *Dicroidium,* is a relic of a warmer age when the country was green – when Antarctica, Africa, South America and Australia were one. The fern was widespread on all the continents that made up Gondwanaland.

20. All but five per cent of the continent lies under a sheet of ice. The Commonwealth Glacier is born in an armchair-like depression or cirque, in the Asgard Range, but it travels only five kilometres before it comes abruptly to an end in the Taylor Valley – one of the few areas in Antarctica inexplicably free of ice. The frontal lobe of the glacier is about 20 metres high.
(Photograph by Antarctic Survey, New Zealand)

21. Long, long ago this rock was soft mud in which many small creatures lived. Now, 370 million years later, the rock is upthrust as a sandstone cliff in the Transantarctic Mountains – too high and too cold for life.
Rocks are monuments to the early history of the continent. Within the hard layers of sediment, fragments of primitive plants have been found, as well as the burrows and tracks of small aquatic animals.
(Photograph by Dr J. McPherson)

22. About 200 years ago sealers began to explore the south. But they were not the first men to dodge between the icebergs. According to Polynesian legend, in the seventh century, canoes reached a place of bitter cold where the sea was covered with white powder and 'things like great white rocks rose high into the sky'.

23. Only the weird humming, creaking, groaning noises of icebergs break the stillness of midnight in the pack. Sea, sun and wind will gradually weather the great towers of ice to tumbled ruins.

24. Was this the way the world looked when the ice ages began?
A blizzard whips snow off the top of a floating ice shelf on the coast of Victoria Land. Some scientists speculate that the Antarctic ice sheet is unstable, that it builds up until it begins to melt at the base, then 'surges' rapidly outwards to form a large floating ice shelf in the Southern Ocean. Antarctic surges, if they in fact occurred, could have been the trigger for the ice ages of the past.

25. Like the shadow of a ghoul, the southern giant petrel follows the scent of death. 'When the boatswain fell off the *Erebus* and could not be saved,' a shipmate reported, 'the giant petrels swooped at him as he struggled to keep afloat.' Like all seabirds, this petrel freely drinks sea-water, and the dribble from its nostril is excess salt being secreted by a gland in its head.

26. Layers of ash blacken Deception Island, from a grumbling volcano which last erupted in 1969. On the highest mountain, slabs of ice were shaken loose, hurtling down in flood and avalanche while the sea hissed steam. The lava flows of that eruption are still visible, the icefields still dingy with cinders and ash.

94

95

96 97

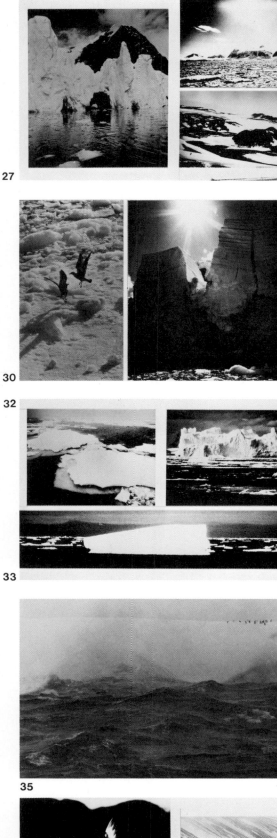

27

28

29

30

31

32

34

33

35

36 37

27. When the sea is rough it makes a resounding roar as it dashes in and out of the gullies of an icebound coastline. Beating against the icy cliffs, gradually eroding the rock and ice, the wash of the waves hollows out caverns, polishes tunnels that stand stark on this unexpectedly calm day.

28. Beyond the Gerlache Strait a line of peaks rises out of the sea. They look near – yet it may take a long time to reach them for the cold air confuses perspectives. There is an almost complete absence of dust in the air of the Antarctic and it has a low moisture content, too. The result is high visibility, and mariners are wary of estimating distances based merely on appearances.

29. 'As we approached land under all studding sail, we perceived a low white line as far as we could see,' said Sir James Clark Ross in 1841. 'It presented an extraordinary appearance, gradually increasing in height as we got nearer to it, and proving at length to be a perpendicular cliff of ice between 100 and 200 feet above sea level, perfectly flat and level at the top.' For 400 kilometres Ross sailed below the icy cliffs without finding break or opening – and even then he had not reached the end, for the Great Ice Barrier stretches some 800 kilometres.

30. Two young kelp gulls flutter down on the pack ice. As man has established permanent settlements on the continent, so some of these birds have taken to overwintering because of the steady supply of scraps thrown out on refuse dumps.

31. The end of a journey. Thousands of years ago, somewhere in the desolate heights of the Antarctic interior, this glacier began a slow crawl to the sea.
According to one estimate, it would take a particle of ice deposited at the Pole of Inaccessibility – the point farthest from the coastline – 100 000 years to travel to the edge of the ice sheet.

32. The left-over rubble of winter – floes crunching and grumbling in the Ross Sea.

33. 'Sunlight at midnight in the pack is perfectly wonderful. One looks out upon endless fields of broken ice, all violet and purple in the low shadows, and all gold and orange and rose red on the broken edges which catch the light. Now and again a penguin cries out in the stillness.' *Edward Wilson, 1910*

34. In 1854, 21 merchant ships reported an amazing sight, a vast body of ice between latitudes 44° and 40° south – in the northern hemisphere Portugal lies within the corresponding latitudes.
The ice mass, probably a group of bergs locked together, was in the form of a hook almost 100 kilometres long by 60 kilometres wide. Driven by winds and ocean currents, icebergs may journey far away from Antarctica. The weathered turrets and battlements of this frozen castle show that it has spent many months at sea.

35. A deep ocean swell washes the smooth slope of an iceberg hundreds of kilometres from the nearest land. The smoothed shape of the ice shows that the berg has been travelling for some time – and at least part of the way the penguins have travelled with it. By using these floating islands as resting-places, the birds extend their feeding ranges.

36. Few Antarctic birds are immune from the attentions of skuas – aggressive attackers that swoop down on unattended nests and young, or overtake and rob other birds in mid-air. The ground near petrel burrows is often strewn with dismembered carcasses of birds killed by skuas. These birds will also scavenge what they can, following ships at sea.
The south polar skua is the only bird ever recorded at the South Pole; the brown skua (above) is found on sub-Antarctic islands.

37. Chinstrap penguins follow a frozen stream between the cinder slopes of Deception Island. An active volcano may not be an ideal nesting ground but breeding space in Antarctica is so hard to come by that the penguins make do with what they can find. After the last eruption some suffered blistered feet rather than relinquish their breeding ground.

169

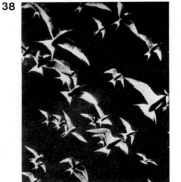

38. Every wind is a highway in the air – an invisible highway well-travelled by the birds. Arctic terns ride the air currents on their annual round trip of 35 000 kilometres between the northern and the southern polar regions. Here, South American terns throng the sky near Tierra del Fuego.

39. An imperial cormorant drops down on the shore of an Antarctic island where it is a resident, fishing adjacent waters. The bird's prominent nasal caruncles vary in colour depending on the season.

40. The noisy trumpeting of hundreds of rockhopper penguins reverberates among the cliffs of Beauchene Island in the Falklands. Nesting close to the penguins are black-browed albatrosses. Once the crews of visiting ships killed thousands of penguins for oil and meat, while egg-hunting wiped out some penguin colonies close to Port Stanley, the only town in the Falklands.
Until recently, November 9th was traditionally devoted to penguin egg-hunting and was a holiday for schoolchildren on the islands.

41. King and gentoo penguins gather at a freshwater stream fed by the sighing cascades of melting summer snow and ice from the mountain valleys on the island of South Georgia. South Georgia is Britain's oldest Antarctic possession but probably was sighted by Amerigo Vespucci in the early sixteenth century.

40 41

42. When Deception Island erupted in 1967, all that remained of the Chilean base was this wreckage of twisted metal. No one was at the base when the volcanic bombs rained down, but five meteorologists at the British base were lucky to escape with their lives.

43. A derelict whaling hut gave shelter to the men during the terrifying chaos of the eruption. Although Deception Island ceased to be a whaling centre in 1931 when factory ships began to process whales at sea, more than 40 years later many reminders of the industry are still found on its shores. This old boat is covered with volcanic cinders.

42
43

44

44. Deception Island's spasms have subsided. For the moment it is safe for visitors to walk along the rim of a crater, looking down on a simmering lake coloured by sulphur. Since this photograph was taken, however, part of the north-facing wall of this crater has collapsed.

45. A bank of snow shows up reindeer which moments before had merged colours with those of tussock grass, moss and rock. The deer have increased on South Georgia since the first 11 animals were introduced to the island by Norwegian whalers 70 years ago. Today thousands of reindeer damage the vulnerable island vegetation. Reindeer have also been established on the archipelago of Kerguelen.

46. Hardy lichens add colour to this composite of grass and rocks on an Antarctic island.

47. There are islands on which men have never landed. Many island peaks have not been climbed. Beaufort Island, in the Ross Sea, is locked within the pack ice all winter. In summer it stands in the path of icebergs calving off the Ross Ice Shelf.
So many ships are wrecked on the rocky shores of sub-Antarctic islands that at one time the New Zealand Government sent an annual relief ship to pick up shipwrecked mariners on Snares, Bounty and Antipodes islands, which lay on the old shipping route from Europe to Australia.

45 46

47

170

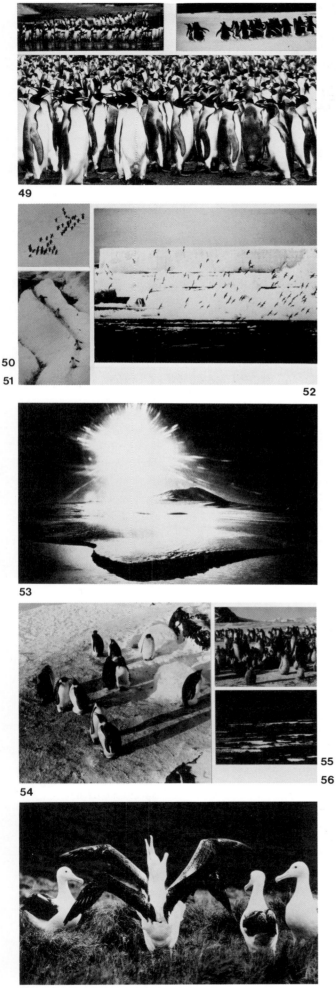

48

49

50
51

52

53

54

55
56

57

48. (top left & right) Penguin stew was regularly featured on Antarctic menus, although it is an acquired taste and Dr Frederick Cook of the de Gerlache expedition in 1898 described penguin meat as being like 'a piece of beef and odiferous codfish and canvas-backed duck roasted in a pot with blood and codliver oil for sauce'.
When the *Gauss* was caught in the ice in 1902 penguins were even used to stoke the furnace of the ship. Thousands of penguins were killed for their oil, their skins made up as rugs or mats. But although all these activities of man affected many colonies, many have recovered and today there is a penguin population explosion. Here crowds of gentoo penguins enter the sea, and return to shore.

49. They may look purposeful, but these king penguins are just standing about on the edge of the breeding colony. Kings make no nest, but hold their single egg on their feet until the chick is ready to hatch. Colonies of more than 10 000 birds are found breeding on sub-Antarctic islands.

50. One blank white space may appear to be much like any other blank white space in Antarctica – if you are a human, that is. Penguins, however, have a fine sense of direction. Adélie penguins have been caught at their nests and then released far away on a different coast – but they were back on their own nests for the next breeding season.

51. Going up . . . and going down. Gentoo penguins have worn paths on the icy slope that lies between their rookery and the sea.
'We drank lime juice and water which sometimes included a suspicious penguin flavour derived from the ice slopes from which our water was quarried,' Apsley Cherry-Garrard reported during Scott's 1910–1912 expedition.

52. With fast wingbeats, then long glides, pintado and Antarctic petrels flicker through the open pack ice. Antarctic petrels and snow petrels are the only birds known to breed deep in the interior of the Antarctic continent. The birds nest together on low, snow-free cliffs, laying their eggs in crevices between the rocks. One colony of Antarctic petrels has been found 250 kilometres from the coast on an isolated peak projecting through the ice sheet.

53. As the shadow of the earth creeps over the horizon, men begin to see each other differently. They turn in upon themselves. To winter in the Antarctic is a long, hard struggle for body and mind. (Photograph by Antarctic Survey, New Zealand)

54. In 1901 British explorers were the first to discover an emperor penguin breeding ground in Antarctica. It was October at the time, the beginning of spring, yet already the eggs had hatched and young birds were sitting on parents' feet. The men were startled, for there could be no doubt the penguins must lay their eggs in the middle of the long polar night. (Photograph by Doug Allan, British Antarctic Survey)

55. The breeding emperors risk an early thaw or a long freeze: if their gamble comes off, the ice of the rookery will not melt back until midsummer when the penguin chicks are old enough to fend for themselves at sea. (Photograph by P.J. Le Morvan)

56. While the emperor males lean together in silent, motionless huddles, each brooding an egg upon its feet, the mother birds are far away on the edge of the pack ice, diving in the dark water, fattening up for their turn at the rookery to care for their newly-hatched youngster.

57. The courtship dance of the royal albatross is accompanied by unmusical shrieks and heavy-footed pirouettes. In sub-adult birds, the performance is one which will be repeated year after year. As they learn attachment to their island and their mate, so they come closer to breeding. There are no hasty marriages in the albatross family.

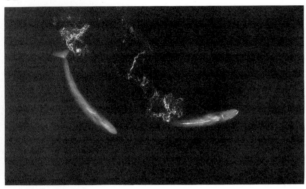

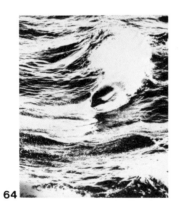

58. The royal albatross – with the wanderer, the greatest of all ocean fliers – lays but a single egg each breeding season. If the egg breaks it is not replaced that year – so each time early sailors collected albatross eggs for food, they wiped out a generation. The ring on the leg of this bird marks it as a study subject.

59. A pair of black-browed albatrosses settles down to the hard work of breeding.

60. The royal albatross builds its nest where there is the space and wind it needs for take-off. In the days of sailing ships, albatrosses were caught on hooked, baited lines and then kept as pets. On deck they lacked the room necessary to become airborne and found themselves trapped as securely as if they were caged.

61. The young black-browed albatross has few enemies. For months it sits on the nest, unguarded, unhidden, but safe. Yet the chick has some defence against intruders. Moments before this picture was taken, the chick ejected a stream of foul-smelling liquid through its beak at the photographer. Some still spatters its down.

62. As soon as a parent black-browed albatross returns to the nest, its downy youngster begs for a meal by coaxing the adult bird to open its beak and regurgitate a pulpy mass of seafood.

63. Blue whales, giants of the world's oceans, seen from the air, their flukes just breaking water. The populations of blue whales have been reduced to the point where the survival of the species is endangered. (Photograph by Russ Kinne)

64. A killer whale breaks the surface in the Ross Sea. Every spring groups of these whales close in on the shores of sub-Antarctic islands – just when the pregnant elephant seals haul out. On Marion Island researchers have shown that the occurrence of killer whales is synchronised to elephant seal movements. When seals are moving about, killer whales patrol close inshore. When winter approaches and the adult elephant seals depart, the killer whales leave the island, too.

65. Once whaling ships carried blacksmiths on board who worked full-time straightening twisted harpoon shafts. A modern whaling fleet operates with precision, but whales are hard to come by. In the Antarctic the main target is now the minke – a whale once thought too small to be worth hunting. This Russian ship in the Bellingshausen Sea has dead minkes alongside.

66. A grotesque reminder of the early days of Antarctic whaling when dead whales were stripped of their blubber and whalebone, and their carcasses cast adrift on the sea. Skeletons and bones were later dumped by the tides on island beaches. Today whalers use every part of the whale.

67. The summer of 1930 – 31 marked a turning-point in Antarctic whaling – the beginning of the possible end of the blue whale. That season a record 30 000 blues were killed to produce a record three million barrels of oil. Oil nobody wanted. The next year most whaling fleets stayed home. 1931 was also the year the whaling station at Deception Island closed down. Today old whale oil casks lie exploded and broken by the island's invading volcanic ash.

68

69

70

71

72 73   74 75

76

77

78

79

80

68. When the United States of America began preparations for rocket probes of Mars and Venus, a team was sent to Antarctica's dry valleys to investigate methods of detecting life in conditions almost as hostile as outer space. This is the only large region of the continent not overwhelmed by sheets of ice.
Although the Upper Victoria Glacier in the Victoria Valley once travelled all the way to the sea, today it stops short on withered brown slopes. The pronounced U-shape of the dry valleys indicates they were once scoured out by large glaciers driving from the polar plateau to the coast. Most of the glacier ice is lost by sublimation, not melting, but some melt-water gives rise to Lake Vida farther down the valley. (Photograph by Dr J. McPherson)

69. A pumice beach on Deception Island makes a strange resting-place for a Weddell seal which normally inhabits the fast-ice. Out of water the Weddell seal is a stout, short-sighted, sleepy animal. Under Antarctica's ice it is a swift, lithe predator. It survives in the fast-ice zone by rasping with its canines and incisors at the ice to make breathing holes. This hard treatment results in the rotten teeth which contribute to the death of older Weddell seals.

70. While crabeaters may be the most numerous seals in the world, they are not easy targets for hunters – and this photograph shows why. Crabeaters live in the most inaccessible region in the world, the Antarctic pack ice. In winter it is a no-man's land, and in summer the crabeaters, which are solitary by nature, are widely scattered on drifting floes.

71. Fur seals gather in crowded rookeries of hundreds and even thousands of animals, all packed closely together on rocky island shores. The early sealers met little resistance as they moved through the harems and one man could club and flay 50 seals in a day. The true Antarctic seals – the crabeaters, Weddells, leopard and Ross seals – were largely protected from the depredations of the sealers by the pack ice.

Danger for penguins usually lurks at sea. But not this time. Here, on one of the Falkland Islands, a sea lion flops rapidly towards a party of rockhopper penguins **(72)**. The birds scatter in disarray, tumbling back into the sea. But one penguin does not move fast enough **(73)**. The sea lion makes a lunge – and its meal is secured. Before swallowing the bird, however, the sea lion tugs at it vigorously **(74)**. In the process, a violent fling sends the penguin towards the water, and the sea lion has to move smartly to retrieve it **(75)**. Sea lions are not found south of the Antarctic Convergence.

76. Little is known about the biology of the leopard seal, for it mates and pups in the impenetrable icefields of the pack. In summer, solitary leopard seals may be seen patrolling near penguin colonies, but birds make up only a third of this seal's somewhat catholic diet.

77. 'Snotter' the early seal hunters called the inflatable trunk of the huge male elephant seal, and they lopped it off, cooked it, and relished it as a titbit.
The largest of all seals, an adult elephant seal bull may weigh three tonnes, a third of this weight being blubber.

78. A crabeater resting on the ice. In summer these animals of the pack move close inshore, and when they move out to sea once more, there are sometimes young animals, 'their noses pointed in the wrong direction', which travel inland. Dead seals have been found 900 metres up in Anarctica's mountains, as far as 60 kilometres from the sea.

79. The silky, blonde, female crabeater seal looks attractive – but get too close and you will find her breath smells like a drainpipe. Crabeaters feed on krill and have specially modified teeth and palates for sieving the shrimplike crustaceans out of the water.

80. This headland at King George Island is stained pink with the guano deposited by krill-eating penguins.

173

81 82

84

83 85

86

88

87 89

90

81. A big quarrel is brewing over this small animal, *Euphausia superba.* Swarms of this euphausiid, otherwise known as krill, are today the target of ships from a number of countries trawling experimentally in the Southern Ocean. While krill is being mooted as the last large unexploited source of food for man, it is also the food of millions of birds, millions of seals, thousands of whales. It is the main link in Antarctic food webs. This specimen lies thrown up on a volcanic beach, cooked by the warmth of the water.

82. The presence of swarms of krill in the Antarctic seas may be detected by satellites hundreds of kilometres above the earth. While swarms appear in surface waters, they more usually lie hidden in slightly deeper layers. Scientists have estimated that large swarms may weigh 100 000 tonnes, but little is known about when krill swarm, where and why. It is crucial that the mysteries of krill biology be solved before the shrimp-like animals are exploited on a large scale.

83. A bedraggled Adélie penguin chick, stained red, leaves little doubt that this bird lives off krill. Until the chick is old enough to go to sea, it is fed on regurgitated krill which its parents collect in off-shore waters.

84. An Adélie penguin parent arriving at its nesting place with a load of krill, is set upon by young demonstrators claiming a share. Despite all the threats and jostling, the adult keeps the food until it hears its own chick calling. Only when it reaches its offspring does it disgorge the meal it is carrying.

85. There is nothing clean and tidy about this Adélie penguin rookery. Nests are placed just one peck apart, and melting snow and squirts of red guano are churned into a stinking quagmire by the passage of penguins.

86. A penguin violates the nesting territory of an irate imperial cormorant.

87. The slopes of Ross Island dwarf two Adélie penguins floating past on a 'growler'. These penguins 'are remarkably stupid', observed Sir James Clark Ross, 'and allow you to approach them so near as to strike them on the head with a bludgeon, and sometimes, if knocked off the ice into the water, will almost immediately leap upon it again as if to attack, but without means of either defence or offence.' The penguins, of course, had never known danger on land. Between man and penguin there has always been misunderstanding.

88. If the inquisitive Adélies were ignorant of danger, the rockhopper penguins certainly gave as good as they got. Plumes bristling, red eyes gleaming, the rockhoppers pecked furiously at the legs of any intruders who tried to pass through their colonies.

89. The projections visible in the beak of the macaroni penguin assist the bird in grasping the euphausiid shrimps which make up its diet.

90. Crabeaters are the most numerous seals in the world – there are an estimated 15 million in the Antarctic pack ice. However, gatherings as large as this one are unusual. It is more common to see twos and threes basking on the floes. The scars visible on some of these seals were once thought to have been inflicted by killer whales. It now appears more likely that leopard seals are to blame.

91. For 19 days out of 20, Antarctica is bleak, desolate, storm-ridden. Yet there are moments when the day is so quiet you can almost hear an icicle form. This tranquil summer pool in the pack lies within an iceberg cave.

92. Returning to camp with a packload of rocks, a geologist treads carefully on a plain of blue-rippled ice. The geologist is a woman – one of the first to participate in fieldwork in Antarctica. In the past 10 years, however, women have ceased to be a rarity in what was once a men-only world. (Photograph by Dr J. McPherson)

93. Below the snowfields and glaciers of Hope Bay, Emilio Marcos Palma was born on 7 January 1978. He was the first child born in Antarctica.

94. The biggest city on the last continent, McMurdo Station, headquarters of American operations on Antarctica. The settlement can house about 1 000 people, and provides every possible mod. con. (Photograph by Dr J. McPherson)

95. 'Welcome to Argentine Antarctica' is the message broadcast across the water by this Argentinian gunboat near the Antarctic Peninsula. But ownership of this region is disputed by Britain, Chile and Argentina.

96. Steam rises around a tourist party on a beach at Deception Island.

97. In 1956 Chile organised the first tourist flight to Antarctica. That was the same year the Adélie penguin numbers began crashing at Cape Royds, the site of Shackleton's 1907 – 09 expedition. The birds had become star attractions to a steady flow of VIP's. Almost every fine day helicopters brought visitors in, scattering penguins with each landing. Some days three, four or five loads of visitors flew in to see the sights. By 1962 penguin numbers had halved. By 1966 Cape Royds was declared out of bounds to everyone – even scientists. Only two years later, however, the tourist invasion of Antarctica began in earnest, and the United States and New Zealand published *Policy Statements on Tourism in Antarctica*. Today Treaty nations try to concentrate tourist landings in special areas where the effects of the visitors can be monitored and assessed before further controls are brought in.

98. 'White-out' is an ever-present threat in Antarctica. This eerie phenomenon is caused by daylight reflected back and forth between snow and an overcast sky, thus obliterating horizons. In a white-out a man can lose himself metres from base. This view of Scott Base was taken during a blizzard. The box-like huts are wired down as protection against gales, and are linked by iron walkways. (Photograph by Dr J. McPherson)

99. Antarctica is a desert with virtually no water. SANAE, the South African scientific base, gets its supply of this critical commodity from snow which is hand-shovelled down a 10-metre chute into a tank that is warmed by the engine rooms below the ice. During blizzards the task of digging the water supply becomes so arduous that even the strongest men are reduced to whimpering, stumbling, cursing figures. Every time the shovel is loaded, the wind whisks the snow away and it seems to take an eternity before the tank is full. (Photograph by K. Cleland)

100. Rough, wind-sculpted *sastrugi* produce a nightmare surface for travel on the Skelton Névé, southern Victoria Land. The photograph was taken at midnight, while the sun was shining 24 hours a day. The man in the photograph, Dr Peter Barrett, made newspaper headlines around the world in 1967 when he chipped a small fragment of a fossil jaw from a peak in the Transantarctic Mountains – the first evidence that vertebrate animals had ever walked Antarctica. (Photograph by Dr J. McPherson)

'Recognizing that it is in the interests of all mankind that Antarctica shall continue forever to be used exclusively for peaceful purposes and shall not become the object of international discord . . .'
Antarctic Treaty, 1959

Index